SUPER EASY EXCEL

Elevate Your Skills and Conquer any Spreadsheet Challenge with
Confidence Through this User-Friendly Guide Designed
for Absolute Beginners

Chet Craig

TABLE OF CONTENTS

1. INTRODUCTION TO EXCEL

Imagine opening a blank spreadsheet for the first time, feeling both curious and a bit daunted by the grid of endless cells stretching out before you. That's where our journey begins. Excel is like a magical toolbox, packed with instruments that can transform how you handle data, solve problems, and even make decisions. Whether you're a student managing class projects, a small business owner tracking expenses, or someone simply looking to organize life a bit better, Excel can be your ally.

So, what exactly is Excel? At its core, Excel is a powerful software developed by Microsoft, designed to help you work with data efficiently. It's like a supercharged version of a ledger or a notebook, where you can input numbers, text, dates, and more, and then manipulate this data to extract meaningful insights. The beauty of Excel lies in its versatility—it can handle anything from the simplest to the most complex tasks.

Let's embark on a quick tour of the Excel interface. When you open Excel, you're greeted with a ribbon at the top, full of tabs like Home, Insert, and Formulas. These tabs house various commands and tools that we'll get familiar with as we progress. Below the ribbon lies the worksheet area, a grid made up of rows and columns. Each rectangle within this grid is a cell, where you can enter data. Cells are the fundamental building blocks of an Excel worksheet, and learning to navigate and utilize them effectively is our first big step.

You'll also notice a formula bar above the grid and a name box to the left. The formula bar is your workspace for crafting formulas that perform calculations or data transformations. The name box shows the reference of the selected cell, helping you keep track of your position within the grid.

Mastering Excel might seem like climbing a mountain, but don't worry—it's all about taking one step at a time. As we delve deeper, you'll learn that Excel is not just about crunching numbers; it's about making your work smarter and more efficient. By the end of this chapter, you'll be comfortable with the Excel environment, ready to start creating, saving, and exploring workbooks. So, let's dive in and unlock the potential that awaits within those tiny cells!

1.1 WHAT IS EXCEL?

Think of Excel as a Swiss Army knife for data. At first glance, it might just seem like a grid of rows and columns, but it's so much more. Excel, developed by Microsoft, is a dynamic spreadsheet program that allows you to organize, format, and calculate data with formulas. It's used in countless industries and professions, from finance to education, and its applications are almost limitless.

Imagine you're planning a family reunion. You've got a list of attendees, their contact information, and the dishes they're bringing. Managing all this information can be cumbersome, but with Excel, it's a breeze. You can input all this data into a spreadsheet, sort it by names, filter it by dishes, and even calculate how many people are bringing dessert. This is just a tiny peek into what Excel can do.

To understand Excel, let's break it down step by step, starting with its basic structure and functionality.

The Spreadsheet Grid

When you open Excel, you're presented with a workbook. Think of a workbook as a book, and each sheet within it as a page. These sheets are called worksheets, and they are made up of a grid of cells. Each cell is like a tiny box where you can input data. The grid is organized into columns labeled with letters (A, B, C, etc.) and rows labeled with numbers (1, 2, 3, etc.). The intersection of a column and a row is a cell, which you can reference by its column letter and row number (e.g., A1, B2).

Entering Data

To start, click on a cell and begin typing. Press Enter to move to the cell below or Tab to move to the cell on the right. This basic data entry is the first step in creating your spreadsheet. You can enter different types of data, including text, numbers, and dates. For example, in planning our family reunion, you might enter names in column A, contact numbers in column B, and dishes in column C.

Formatting Cells

Formatting makes your data readable and visually appealing. You can format cells to change their appearance without altering the data itself. For instance, you can bold text, change the font size, or adjust the alignment. This is done through the Home tab on the Ribbon—the toolbar at the top of the Excel window.

Imagine you want the header row (names, contact numbers, dishes) to stand out. You can select the entire row, then use the formatting tools to make the text bold and increase its size. You can also apply borders to the cells to make them more distinct.

Using Formulas

One of the most powerful features of Excel is its ability to perform calculations using formulas. A formula in Excel always begins with an equals sign (=). For instance, if you want to add numbers in cells A1 and A2, you would click on an empty cell and type =A1+A2. Press Enter, and Excel will display the result.

Formulas can be simple arithmetic, like addition or subtraction, or they can be more complex, involving functions like SUM, AVERAGE, and COUNT. These functions allow you to perform quick calculations on a range of cells. For example, to add all the numbers in a column from A1 to A10, you would use the SUM function: =SUM(A1:A10).

Sorting and Filtering Data

Excel makes it easy to organize your data by sorting and filtering. Sorting arranges your data in a specific order, either ascending or descending. Filtering allows you to display only the data that meets certain criteria.

For instance, if you want to sort your family reunion list alphabetically by name, you would select the column with the names and use the Sort function in the Data tab. If you only want to see who's bringing desserts, you can apply a filter to the dish column and select "desserts" from the dropdown menu.

Creating Charts

Visualizing data with charts helps to make sense of numbers and patterns. Excel offers various chart types like bar charts, pie charts, and line charts. Creating a chart is straightforward: select the data you want to visualize, go to the Insert tab, and choose the type of chart you need.

Suppose you want to see the distribution of dishes at the family reunion. You can highlight the dish column and create a pie chart. This visual representation makes it easy to see which types of dishes are most common at a glance.

PivotTables

PivotTables are a powerful tool for summarizing large amounts of data. They allow you to reorganize and summarize data without altering the original dataset. You can quickly analyze trends and patterns.

Imagine you have a detailed list of all family members attending multiple reunions over the years. A PivotTable can help you summarize attendance by year, showing you trends in participation.

Real-Time Collaboration

Excel's real-time collaboration feature allows multiple users to work on the same workbook simultaneously. This is especially useful for team projects or family planning where input from multiple people is required.

By sharing your workbook online, family members can update their contact details or dish contributions, and everyone will see the changes instantly. This keeps everyone on the same page and makes coordination smoother.

Practical Tips

- **Always save your work frequently**: Excel has an AutoSave feature, but it's good practice to manually save your work regularly.
- **Use descriptive names for your columns**: This makes it easier to understand your data at a glance.
- **Keep your data clean**: Avoid leaving blank rows or columns as they can interfere with data analysis tools like PivotTables.
- **Learn keyboard shortcuts**: They can significantly speed up your workflow. For example, Ctrl+C to copy and Ctrl+V to paste.

Excel is an incredibly versatile tool that can simplify your life in many ways, from personal projects like planning a family reunion to professional tasks like managing business finances. By understanding the basic components and functionalities—such as data entry, formatting, formulas, sorting, and chart creation—you're laying the foundation for becoming an Excel pro.

As we delve deeper into this book, you'll discover how to harness the full power of Excel. You'll learn not just how to input and organize data, but how to use Excel's advanced features to analyze and present your information in compelling ways. So, take a deep breath and dive in with confidence. Excel is a skill that will pay dividends in efficiency and productivity, making your tasks easier and your outcomes more precise. Welcome to the world of Excel, where the potential is as vast as the grid itself.

1.2 NAVIGATING THE EXCEL INTERFACE

When you first open Excel, the interface might look like a complex dashboard of buttons, tabs, and grids. But don't worry; we're going to break it down step-by-step, making it easy to understand and navigate. Think of the Excel interface as your cockpit, with each component designed to help you fly through your data tasks efficiently.

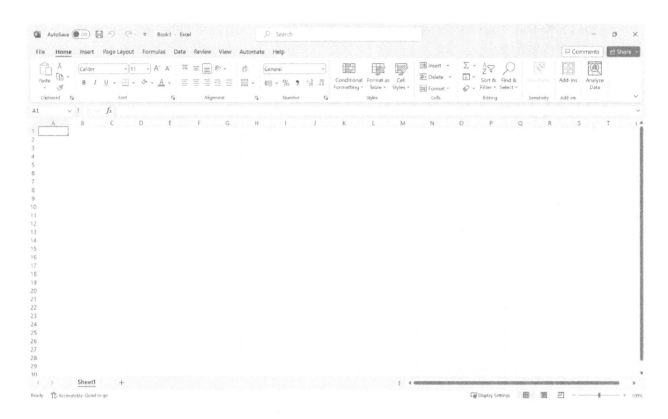

The Ribbon: Your Command Center

At the top of the Excel window, you'll find the Ribbon. This is your main control panel, housing all the tools and commands you need. The Ribbon is organized into several tabs, each grouping related commands together. Let's take a closer look at some of the key tabs:

- **Home**: This is where you'll find the basic tools for formatting cells, managing clipboard actions (cut, copy, paste), and adjusting font and alignment. Imagine you're preparing a report card; you'll use the Home tab to format text, align numbers, and make the sheet look presentable.

- **Insert**: Use this tab when you want to add elements like tables, charts, pictures, and shapes. Think of it like decorating a cake with various toppings to make it more appealing.

- **Page Layout**: Here, you can adjust the appearance of your worksheet for printing. It's like setting up your printer for a perfect printout, ensuring margins, orientation, and size are just right.

- **Formulas**: This tab contains functions and tools to create and manage your formulas. Whether you're calculating monthly expenses or determining the average score in a class, this is your go-to spot.

- **Data**: This is where you manage data tasks like sorting, filtering, and data analysis. Picture yourself organizing a large music collection by genre, artist, or year.

- **Review**: For tasks like spell check, adding comments, and protecting your workbook, the Review tab is essential. It's like having a second pair of eyes to review and annotate your work.
- **View**: This tab lets you control how you see your workbook, including zooming and arranging multiple windows. It's like adjusting your workspace to be as comfortable and efficient as possible.

Quick Access Toolbar

Just above the Ribbon, you'll notice a small toolbar. This is the Quick Access Toolbar, where you can place your most frequently used commands for easy access. By default, it includes Save, Undo, and Redo buttons. You can customize it to include other commands you use often, like Print Preview or New Workbook, making your workflow faster and smoother.

The Workbook: Your Canvas

In the center of the interface is the workbook area, your main workspace. A workbook is like a book, with multiple sheets or pages. Each sheet within the workbook is called a worksheet. Worksheets are where you input and manipulate your data.

- **Sheets**: Each worksheet is a grid of cells organized into columns (labeled A, B, C, etc.) and rows (labeled 1, 2, 3, etc.). The intersection of a column and a row is a cell, where you enter data. For example, cell B3 is where column B and row 3 meet.
- **Tabs**: At the bottom, you'll see tabs for each sheet in your workbook. You can add new sheets, rename them, move them around, or delete them as needed.

The Formula Bar: Your Input Line

Just below the Ribbon, you'll find the Formula Bar. This is where you enter and edit data or formulas in the selected cell. It's like the text box on a search engine, but instead of searching the web, you're inputting and editing data.

For example, if you click on cell C5 and type =SUM(A1:A4) in the Formula Bar, you're telling Excel to add up the values in cells A1 through A4 and display the result in C5. The Formula Bar shows exactly what you're entering, making it easier to review and correct.

The Name Box: Your Locator

To the left of the Formula Bar is the Name Box. This shows the reference of the currently selected cell (like A1, B2, etc.). It's also where you can name ranges of cells for easy reference. For instance, if you select cells A1 to A10 and name this range "Sales," you can use this name in formulas instead of the cell references, making your formulas easier to understand and manage.

Navigation Pane: Finding Your Way

On the left side, you might see a Navigation Pane, especially if you have additional features like add-ins or multiple sheets. This pane helps you jump quickly to different parts of your workbook or access specific tools and options.

Status Bar: Your Information Center

At the bottom of the Excel window, the Status Bar provides useful information about your workbook. It shows details like the average, count, and sum of selected cells, as well as the current view mode and zoom level. It's like having a dashboard that gives you instant feedback on your data and actions.

Practical Tips for Navigation

- **Moving Around**: Use the arrow keys to move from cell to cell, or click directly on a cell with your mouse. For larger jumps, use Ctrl + arrow keys to move to the edge of the data region.
- **Selecting Cells**: Click and drag to select a range of cells, or use Shift + arrow keys for precise selection. Ctrl + click allows you to select non-adjacent cells.
- **Finding Commands**: If you're unsure where to find a command, use the Tell Me feature (light bulb icon on the Ribbon). Type what you're looking for, and Excel will guide you.

Real-World Example: Creating a Budget

Let's bring this all together with a real-world example. Imagine you're creating a monthly budget. Start by opening a new workbook. Use the Home tab to enter headers like "Income," "Expenses," and "Savings" in the first row. Format these headers to stand out.

Next, move to the Insert tab to add a table for your data entries. This helps organize your numbers neatly. In the Formula Bar, use basic formulas to calculate totals and balances. The Data tab will help you sort and filter your expenses to see where you're spending the most.

Customize your Quick Access Toolbar with commands like Save and Print Preview, ensuring you can quickly save your progress and review your layout. Use the View tab to adjust how your worksheet appears on your screen, making it easier to navigate large amounts of data.

Navigating the Excel interface might seem complex at first, but with a little practice, it becomes second nature. The Ribbon, Quick Access Toolbar, workbook area, Formula Bar, Name Box, and Status Bar are your main tools. Each has a specific role, helping you perform tasks efficiently and effectively. By understanding these components, you're well on your way to mastering Excel and unlocking its full potential.

Remember, Excel is designed to make your data tasks easier and more efficient. Whether you're managing a budget, analyzing data, or simply organizing information, getting comfortable with the interface is the first step towards becoming an Excel pro. So, take your time exploring these tools and features, and soon you'll be navigating Excel like a seasoned expert.

1.3 BASIC EXCEL TERMINOLOGY

Diving into Excel can feel like learning a new language, but once you get the hang of its terminology, everything becomes much clearer. Let's take a friendly walk through the basic terms you'll encounter as you start your journey with Excel. Think of this as getting to know the lay of the land before setting off on an adventure.

Workbook and Worksheet

Imagine a workbook as a physical book. Just like a book contains multiple pages, an Excel workbook contains multiple worksheets. Each worksheet is like a page in that book, providing a space where you can enter and manipulate data. When you open Excel, you're opening a workbook, which is a file with the extension .xlsx.

Cells and Ranges

Cells are the fundamental building blocks of an Excel worksheet. Each cell is like a tiny box where you can enter data, such as numbers, text, or formulas. Cells are identified by their column letter and row number. For example, the cell at the intersection of column B and row 3 is called cell B3.

A range is a group of cells. Ranges are referenced by the cell in the upper-left corner and the cell in the lower-right corner of the block. For example, the range from cell A1 to cell B3 is written as A1
. Understanding how to reference ranges is crucial for performing calculations and creating charts.

Columns and Rows

Columns and rows form the grid of a worksheet. Columns are vertical and labeled with letters (A, B, C, etc.), while rows are horizontal and labeled with numbers (1, 2, 3, etc.). The combination of columns and rows creates cells, where your data lives.

The Ribbon and Tabs

The Ribbon is the toolbar at the top of the Excel window, filled with tabs like Home, Insert, and Data. Each tab contains groups of related commands. For instance, the Home tab includes options for formatting cells, while the Insert tab lets you add charts, tables, and other elements.

Formula Bar and Name Box

The Formula Bar is located above the worksheet grid and displays the contents of the selected cell. This is where you can enter or edit data and formulas. Directly to the left of the Formula Bar is the Name Box, which shows the reference of the active cell and can also be used to name and navigate to ranges.

Formulas and Functions

Formulas are equations that perform calculations on your data. Every formula in Excel starts with an equals sign (=). For example, to add the values in cells A1 and A2, you would enter =A1+A2 in another cell.

Functions are predefined formulas in Excel that simplify complex calculations. Functions like SUM, AVERAGE, and COUNT are essential tools for data analysis. To use a function, you start with an equals sign, followed by the function name and its arguments in parentheses. For example, =SUM(A1:A10) adds up all the values from A1 to A10.

Cell References

Cell references are the way you refer to the cells in your formulas. There are three types of cell references:

- **Relative**: These change when a formula is copied to another cell. For example, if you copy the formula =A1+B1 from cell C1 to cell C2, it will adjust to =A2+B2.
- **Absolute**: These remain constant, no matter where the formula is copied. An absolute reference is indicated by dollar signs, like A1.
- **Mixed**: These combine relative and absolute references, such as $A1 or A$1.

Understanding these references is key to creating flexible and accurate formulas.

Sorting and Filtering

Sorting arranges your data in a specific order, while filtering allows you to display only the data that meets certain criteria. For instance, you can sort a list of names alphabetically or filter a list of sales transactions to show only those above a certain amount. These tools help you manage and analyze your data more effectively.

Charts and Graphs

Charts are visual representations of your data, making it easier to understand and analyze. Excel offers various chart types, such as bar charts, line charts, and pie charts. Creating a chart involves selecting your data and choosing the appropriate chart type from the Insert tab.

PivotTables

PivotTables are powerful tools for summarizing large amounts of data. They allow you to reorganize and analyze data dynamically. For example, a PivotTable can help you summarize sales data by region, product, or salesperson, providing insights into your business performance.

Data Validation

Data validation is a feature that helps you control the type of data entered into a cell. For instance, you can set a rule that only allows numbers between 1 and 100 in a specific range of cells. This helps ensure the accuracy and consistency of your data.

Real-World Example: Planning a Project

Let's say you're planning a community event. You start by opening a new workbook and naming it "Event Planning". Your first worksheet is for the guest list. In columns A and B, you enter names and contact details. You format the headers using the Home tab to make them bold.

Next, you need to keep track of tasks and deadlines. On a new worksheet, you list tasks in column A and deadlines in column B. You can use the SUM function to calculate the total number of tasks or the COUNTIF function to count tasks completed by a certain date.

To visualize your budget, you create a chart. In a new worksheet, you list expenses in column A and amounts in column B. Using the Insert tab, you select a bar chart to display your expenses clearly.

As you progress, you might need to summarize attendee information or task statuses. Creating a PivotTable helps you see at a glance how many guests have confirmed or how many tasks are pending.

Grasping these basic Excel terms sets the foundation for everything you'll do in this powerful tool. A workbook is your canvas, filled with worksheets that house your data in cells. Columns and rows organize your information, while the Ribbon and tabs provide the tools you need to manipulate and analyze it.

Formulas and functions enable you to perform calculations, and understanding cell references ensures your formulas are accurate and flexible. Sorting, filtering, and creating charts help you make sense of your data, while PivotTables provide powerful ways to summarize and analyze large datasets. Data validation ensures the integrity of your information.

With these terms under your belt, you're ready to dive deeper into Excel, confident in your ability to navigate its features and harness its full potential. As we continue, you'll learn to apply these concepts to real-world scenarios, transforming your data into actionable insights and effective presentations. So, take a deep breath, and let's continue our journey into the world of Excel with a solid understanding of its basic terminology.

2. GETTING STARTED WITH EXCEL

Picture yourself opening Excel for the first time, eager yet uncertain about what to do next. You've heard of its capabilities, from simple calculations to complex data analysis, but the initial screen feels like a blank canvas waiting for your masterpiece. This chapter is your friendly guide, easing you into the world of Excel by focusing on the basics: creating and saving workbooks, entering and editing data, and understanding worksheets.

Think of Excel as your digital workspace where each workbook represents a new project. Whether you're planning a budget, tracking a workout routine, or organizing a school event, everything starts with creating a workbook. Imagine this workbook as a binder filled with sheets of paper, each one a worksheet where you can jot down, calculate, and visualize your data.

We'll begin by navigating through the simple steps of creating a new workbook. It's like opening a fresh notebook, ready for your ideas and numbers. You'll learn how to save your work, ensuring that your data is secure and accessible whenever you need it. Saving frequently becomes a habit, a safeguard against unexpected interruptions. Next, we dive into the essence of Excel: entering and editing data. Imagine filling in a guest list for a party, where each cell in a worksheet is a slot for a guest's name, contact information, or dietary preference. You'll see how easy it is to adjust entries, correct mistakes, and ensure everything is perfectly organized.

Finally, we explore the structure of worksheets. Think of a worksheet as a playground for your data, with cells forming the grid where your information lives. Understanding how to navigate and manipulate this grid is crucial for your Excel journey.

By the end of this chapter, you'll be comfortable creating workbooks, entering data, and understanding the layout of worksheets. These foundational skills will set you up for success, making the more advanced features of Excel accessible and manageable. Let's get started, and soon you'll see how Excel can transform your data into something meaningful and powerful.

2.1 CREATING AND SAVING WORKBOOKS

Imagine you've just opened Excel, a blank canvas ready to be filled with your data adventures. The first step in our journey is creating and saving a workbook. Think of a workbook as your project binder, with each worksheet acting as a page where your data stories unfold. This section will guide you through the process, ensuring you start on the right foot.

Creating a Workbook

Creating a new workbook in Excel is as simple as opening a blank notebook. Here's how to do it step-by-step:

1. **Open Excel**: When you launch Excel, you're greeted with the Start screen. This screen provides various templates and options, but for now, we'll focus on creating a blank workbook.
2. **Select Blank Workbook**: Click on the "Blank Workbook" option. This opens a new, empty workbook, ready for your data.

You've just created your first workbook! It's like having a fresh sheet of paper to start sketching your ideas. Now, let's look at the components you'll interact with.

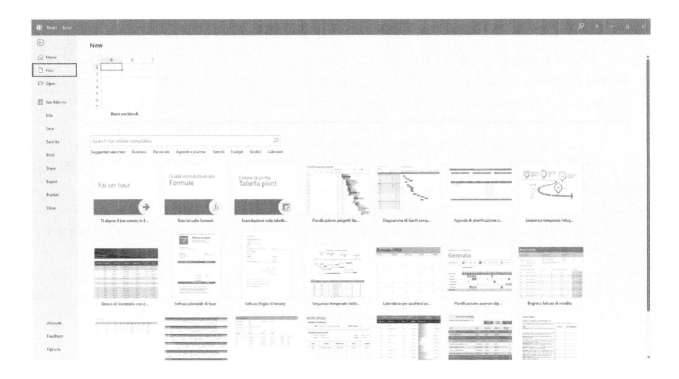

Understanding the Workbook Layout

Your new workbook consists of worksheets, which are the individual pages within your project binder. Each worksheet is a grid of cells organized into columns and rows.

- **Columns**: These run vertically and are labeled with letters (A, B, C, etc.).
- **Rows**: These run horizontally and are labeled with numbers (1, 2, 3, etc.).
- **Cells**: The intersection of a column and a row, such as A1 or B2, where you enter data.

You can add more worksheets to your workbook by clicking the "+" icon at the bottom next to the existing sheet tabs. This allows you to organize different sets of data within the same project binder.

Naming Your Workbook

Before you dive into entering data, it's a good idea to save and name your workbook. Naming your workbook helps you identify it easily among other files. Here's how:

1. **Click on File**: This is located in the upper-left corner of the Excel window.
2. **Select Save As**: This opens a dialog box where you can choose the location to save your workbook.
3. **Enter a Name**: Type a meaningful name for your workbook in the "File Name" field. For example, "Family Budget 2024" or "Project Timeline Q1".
4. **Choose the Location**: Decide where you want to save the file on your computer or cloud storage.
5. **Click Save**: Your workbook is now saved with a name, making it easy to find and recognize.

Saving Your Workbook

Saving your work frequently is crucial to prevent data loss. Excel offers multiple ways to save your workbook:

- **Quick Save**: Simply click the disk icon on the Quick Access Toolbar or press Ctrl+S on your keyboard.
- **Save As**: Use this option when you want to save a copy of your workbook under a different name or location. This is useful for creating versions of your work.

Imagine you're working on a monthly budget. As you enter expenses and incomes, you'll want to save your progress regularly. If you decide to create a new version for a different month, you can use "Save As" to save the current workbook as "February Budget 2024" while keeping the original file intact.

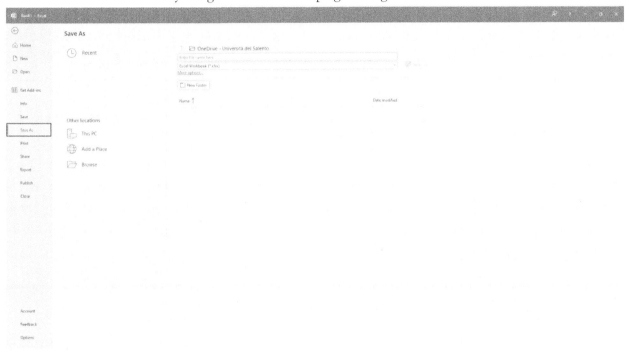

Practical Tips for Saving Workbooks

Here are some practical tips to help you manage your workbooks efficiently:

- **AutoSave**: If you're using Excel 365 and have your workbook saved in OneDrive or SharePoint, AutoSave is a feature that automatically saves your work as you make changes. This provides peace of mind and reduces the risk of data loss.
- **Version History**: In cloud storage like OneDrive, you can access previous versions of your workbook. This is useful if you need to revert to an earlier state.
- **File Formats**: Excel allows you to save your workbook in various formats such as .xlsx, .xls, and .csv. The default format is .xlsx, which supports all Excel features.

Real-World Example: Managing a Small Business

Let's put this into a real-world context. Imagine you run a small bakery, and you want to track your monthly expenses and sales. Here's how you might set up your workbook:

1. **Create a New Workbook**: Open Excel and select "Blank Workbook".
2. **Name Your Workbook**: Save it as "Bakery Finances 2024".
3. **Set Up Worksheets**: Rename the first sheet to "January" by right-clicking the sheet tab and selecting "Rename". Add new sheets for each month of the year.
4. **Enter Data**: In each worksheet, create columns for Date, Item, Expense, and Sales. Start entering your daily transactions.

As you update your workbook with daily sales and expenses, you'll save your work regularly. At the end of each month, you can use "Save As" to create a version of your workbook named "Bakery Finances January 2024" and then continue updating the main workbook for the next month.

Creating and saving workbooks is the foundational step in using Excel effectively. It's like setting up your workspace before starting a project. By understanding how to create a workbook, navigate its layout, and save your progress, you ensure that your data is well-organized and secure.

As we move forward, these skills will be the bedrock upon which you build more complex and powerful Excel tasks. Whether you're managing personal finances, planning events, or running a small business, mastering the basics of workbooks will give you the confidence to tackle any data challenge that comes your way. So go ahead, create your first workbook, and save it with pride. You've taken the first step in your Excel journey, and many more exciting discoveries await!

2.2 ENTERING AND EDITING DATA

Entering and editing data in Excel is like filling in the blanks of a detailed form. Each cell is a blank slate, ready to store information, calculations, or instructions. Imagine you're organizing a list of guests for a wedding, managing your household budget, or tracking sales for a small business. This chapter will guide you through the steps to enter and edit data efficiently, making Excel an indispensable tool in your daily tasks.

Entering Data

The first step to using Excel is entering data into the cells. Here's a simple guide to get you started:

1. **Select a Cell**: Click on a cell where you want to enter data. This cell is now active, indicated by a thick border around it.
2. **Type Your Data**: Begin typing. This could be text (like names), numbers (like quantities), or dates.
3. **Confirm Entry**: Press Enter to move down to the next cell, or press Tab to move to the next cell on the right.

Imagine you're planning a family reunion and need to list everyone's names, contact information, and what dish they're bringing. Start by entering "Name" in cell A1, "Contact" in B1, and "Dish" in C1. Then, under these headers, input the relevant information for each family member.

Editing Data

Sometimes you need to correct or update the data you've entered. Editing data in Excel is straightforward:

1. **Select the Cell**: Click on the cell you want to edit.
2. **Edit Directly**: You can start typing to overwrite the current content or click in the Formula Bar to edit the existing data.
3. **Press Enter**: After making your changes, press Enter to confirm.

Let's say you entered a wrong phone number for Aunt Mary. Click on her contact cell, correct the number in the Formula Bar, and press Enter. The change is saved immediately.

Practical Tips for Entering and Editing Data

- **AutoFill**: This feature helps you quickly fill cells with repetitive or sequential data. For example, if you type "January" in a cell and drag the fill handle (a small square at the cell's bottom-right corner), Excel will automatically fill in the subsequent months.
- **Undo and Redo**: Made a mistake? Use Ctrl+Z to undo your last action. Changed your mind? Ctrl+Y will redo it.
- **Copy and Paste**: Copy data using Ctrl+C and paste it with Ctrl+V. This saves time when dealing with large amounts of data.

Using Real-World Examples

Let's consider another real-world example: managing a household budget. Create a new worksheet with columns for "Date," "Description," "Amount," and "Category." Under these headers, start entering your expenses and income.

- **Date**: Enter the date of the transaction.
- **Description**: Enter what the transaction was for, like "Grocery" or "Electric Bill."
- **Amount**: Enter the amount spent or received.
- **Category**: Categorize your transactions, such as "Food," "Utilities," or "Salary."

Formatting Your Data

Formatting makes your data more readable and visually appealing. Here's how you can format your data in Excel:

1. **Select the Cells**: Click and drag to highlight the cells you want to format.
2. **Use the Ribbon**: On the Home tab, you'll find various formatting options like font size, bold, italics, and cell color.
3. **Apply Formats**: Click the desired formatting options. For example, you can bold your headers or apply a currency format to your Amount column.

Practical Tips for Formatting Data

- **Wrap Text**: If your data doesn't fit in a cell, use the Wrap Text feature in the Home tab to display it on multiple lines within the same cell.

- **Adjust Column Width**: Double-click the boundary of a column header to auto-fit the width to the content.
- **Number Formats**: Use predefined number formats like Currency, Percentage, or Date to standardize how numbers appear.

Real-World Example: Sales Tracking

Consider a small business tracking monthly sales. Create a worksheet with columns for "Date," "Product," "Units Sold," and "Revenue." Input your sales data regularly.

1. **Date**: Enter the sale date.
2. **Product**: Enter the product name.
3. **Units Sold**: Enter the number of units sold.
4. **Revenue**: Enter the total revenue from the sale.

To keep your data organized and visually clear, format the Revenue column as currency and use bold text for the header row.

Data Validation

To ensure accuracy, you can use data validation. This restricts the type of data entered into a cell.

1. **Select the Cells**: Highlight the cells you want to validate.
2. **Go to Data Tab**: Click on the Data tab, then Data Validation.
3. **Set Criteria**: Define the criteria for valid entries. For instance, you might only allow numbers between 1 and 100.

If you're managing a list of student grades, you can use data validation to ensure that only numbers between 0 and 100 are entered in the "Grade" column.

Practical Tips for Data Validation

- **Drop-Down Lists**: Create drop-down lists for categories or predefined options. This reduces errors and speeds up data entry.
- **Input Messages and Error Alerts**: Add messages to guide users when they enter data, and error alerts to notify them of invalid entries.

Entering and editing data in Excel is the foundation of creating meaningful and organized information. Whether you're planning a family event, managing personal finances, or tracking business sales, mastering these basic skills is crucial.

By practicing entering data, editing mistakes, and using formatting and validation tools, you'll find that Excel becomes a powerful ally in your daily tasks. Remember to save your work frequently, use shortcuts to streamline your workflow, and always double-check your data for accuracy.

With these skills under your belt, you're well on your way to becoming proficient in Excel. So go ahead, start entering your data with confidence, and watch as your information transforms into valuable insights and organized records. The more you practice, the more intuitive and powerful Excel will become in your hands.

2.3 UNDERSTANDING EXCEL WORKSHEETS

Imagine opening an Excel workbook and seeing a blank canvas filled with tiny rectangular boxes. These boxes are called cells, and they make up what we call a worksheet. Understanding how to navigate and utilize these worksheets is key to mastering Excel. Think of each worksheet as a separate room in your house, each with its own purpose and functionality, but all part of a bigger picture—your workbook.

The Structure of an Excel Worksheet

An Excel worksheet is a grid composed of columns and rows. Columns run vertically and are labeled with letters (A, B, C, etc.), while rows run horizontally and are numbered (1, 2, 3, etc.). The intersection of a column and a row forms a cell, which is the basic unit where you enter data.

For example, the cell where column A meets row 1 is referred to as A1. This simple structure allows you to organize data systematically and refer to specific points easily. Each cell can contain different types of data, such as text, numbers, dates, or formulas.

Navigating the Worksheet

Navigating through an Excel worksheet is similar to walking through different rooms in a house. Here are some tips to move around efficiently:

1. **Using the Mouse**: Click on any cell to make it active. The active cell is highlighted by a thicker border.
2. **Arrow Keys**: Use the arrow keys on your keyboard to move up, down, left, or right between cells.
3. **Scroll Bars**: Use the horizontal and vertical scroll bars to move to different parts of the worksheet, especially useful for large datasets.
4. **Name Box**: Located to the left of the Formula Bar, you can type a cell reference (like B10) and press Enter to jump directly to that cell.

Imagine you're managing a project timeline. The ability to quickly navigate to a specific task or date helps you stay organized and efficient.

Selecting Cells and Ranges

Selecting cells or ranges of cells is fundamental to performing tasks like formatting, copying, or creating charts. Here's how you can do it:

- **Single Cell**: Click on a cell to select it.
- **Range of Cells**: Click and drag from one cell to another to select a block of cells. For instance, dragging from A1 to B5 selects all cells in that range.
- **Non-Adjacent Cells**: Hold down the Ctrl key while clicking on each cell or range you want to select. This is useful for formatting or analyzing specific, separate pieces of data.

Entering Data

Entering data into a worksheet is straightforward. Click on a cell and start typing. Press Enter to move to the cell below or Tab to move to the next cell on the right. You can enter various types of data:

- **Text**: Useful for headers or labels, like "Name" or "Product."

- **Numbers**: Essential for calculations, such as sales figures or quantities.
- **Dates**: Important for tracking timelines or deadlines.
- **Formulas**: Allow you to perform calculations or logical operations, like =SUM(A1:A10) to add up a column of numbers.

Editing Data

To edit the content of a cell, double-click on the cell or click once and make changes in the Formula Bar. Press Enter to save the changes. This process is similar to editing text in a word processor, making it easy to correct errors or update information.

Formatting Cells

Formatting makes your data more readable and visually appealing. Here's a step-by-step guide to basic formatting:

1. **Select the Cells**: Highlight the cells you want to format.
2. **Use the Ribbon**: Go to the Home tab on the Ribbon.
3. **Apply Formats**: You can change the font, size, color, and alignment of the text. Use options like bold, italics, and underline to emphasize important data.

Imagine you're preparing a financial report. Formatting headers in bold and different colors helps to distinguish between various sections, making the report easier to read and understand.

Practical Tips for Working with Worksheets

- **Freeze Panes**: Keep headers visible while scrolling through large datasets. Go to View > Freeze Panes and choose the appropriate option.
- **Insert and Delete Rows/Columns**: Right-click on a row or column header and choose Insert or Delete to manage the structure of your worksheet.
- **Rename Sheets**: Double-click on a sheet tab at the bottom to rename it. Use descriptive names like "January Sales" or "Project Plan" to stay organized.
- **Move or Copy Sheets**: Right-click on a sheet tab and select Move or Copy. This is helpful for duplicating templates or organizing data across multiple sheets.

Real-World Example: Planning an Event

Let's say you're planning a community event. Start by creating a worksheet to track tasks, deadlines, and responsibilities. In columns A, B, and C, enter headers like "Task," "Deadline," and "Assigned To."

1. **Enter Data**: Fill in each row with specific tasks, deadlines, and the names of team members responsible.
2. **Format Headers**: Highlight the header row and apply bold and color formatting to make it stand out.
3. **Freeze Panes**: Freeze the header row so it remains visible as you scroll through your list of tasks.
4. **Insert Columns**: Add additional columns if needed, such as "Status" to track progress.

By structuring your data in this way, you can easily manage and update your event plan, ensuring nothing falls through the cracks.

Understanding Excel worksheets is like mastering the blueprint of a complex structure. Each component, from cells to columns and rows, plays a critical role in organizing and analyzing your data. By mastering navigation, selection, data entry, and formatting, you lay the foundation for more advanced Excel tasks.

Whether you're managing personal projects, professional tasks, or collaborative efforts, knowing how to effectively use worksheets will enhance your efficiency and accuracy. Practice these basics, and soon you'll find yourself navigating Excel with ease, turning data into meaningful insights and well-organized information. The journey with Excel begins here, and with each step, you'll discover new ways to make this powerful tool work for you.

3. FORMATTING CELLS AND DATA

Imagine you've just created a new Excel worksheet, filled it with data, and now you're staring at a sea of numbers and text. It feels a bit overwhelming, doesn't it? This is where formatting comes to the rescue, transforming your raw data into something that is not only functional but also visually appealing. Think of formatting as the art of Excel, where you can turn a basic spreadsheet into a masterpiece of clarity and professionalism.

Formatting cells and data isn't just about making things look pretty—though that's certainly a part of it. It's about enhancing readability, emphasizing key information, and organizing your data in a way that makes sense. Whether you're preparing a financial report, organizing a project timeline, or simply managing your household budget, the way you present your data can make a world of difference.

In this chapter, we'll explore the various tools and techniques for formatting in Excel. From applying cell styles and custom number formats to using conditional formatting for dynamic data visualization, you'll learn how to make your spreadsheets not only look good but also work better for you.

Imagine you're presenting a sales report to your team. A well-formatted spreadsheet can highlight key metrics, make trends easier to spot, and ensure that your data tells a compelling story. By the end of this chapter, you'll be equipped with the skills to turn any ordinary spreadsheet into a clear, professional document that communicates your data effectively.

So, let's dive in and start painting with data. With the right formatting techniques, you'll transform your spreadsheets from simple tables of information into powerful tools for decision-making and communication.

3.1 APPLYING CELL STYLES AND FORMATTING

Imagine you've just entered your data into an Excel worksheet. It's all there, but it looks like a jumble of numbers and text. This is where applying cell styles and formatting comes into play, transforming your raw data into a visually appealing and easily understandable spreadsheet. Think of formatting as adding the final touches to a painting—it makes the details stand out and the overall picture clearer.

Getting Started with Cell Styles

Cell styles in Excel are like pre-set outfits for your data. They allow you to quickly apply a consistent look to cells that match the overall theme of your document. Here's how you can start using them:

1. **Select the Cells**: Highlight the cells you want to format.
2. **Open Cell Styles**: Go to the Home tab on the Ribbon and click on "Cell Styles" in the Styles group.
3. **Choose a Style**: A gallery of styles will appear. These include titles, headings, and various accent styles. Click on the one that suits your needs.

For instance, if you have a table of monthly expenses, you might use a bold style for the header row and a lighter style for the data cells. This helps differentiate the headings from the data, making your table easier to read.

Customizing Cell Formatting

Beyond the preset styles, you can customize the appearance of individual cells or ranges to better suit your needs. Here's a step-by-step guide to applying custom formatting:

1. **Font and Alignment**: Select the cells you want to format. In the Home tab, you'll find options to change the font, size, color, and alignment. For example, you might center-align headers and left-align data entries for a cleaner look.

2. **Borders and Shading**: Adding borders and shading can help separate different sections of your data. Select your cells, then use the "Borders" and "Fill Color" options in the Home tab to apply these styles. Borders can outline your data, while shading can highlight important rows or columns.

3. **Number Formats**: Excel offers a variety of number formats to display your data appropriately. Select your cells, go to the Number group in the Home tab, and choose from options like General, Number, Currency, Date, or Percentage. For example, if you're tracking sales, use the Currency format to clearly show monetary values.

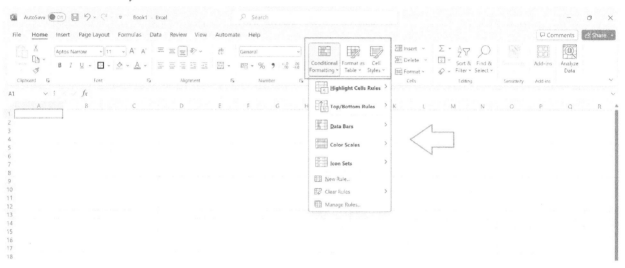

Practical Tips for Effective Formatting

- **Consistency is Key**: Use the same font, size, and color for similar types of data. This consistency helps readers understand and compare information quickly.

- **Highlight Important Data**: Use bold, italics, or colors sparingly to draw attention to key figures or headings. For example, if you have a summary row showing total expenses, making it bold and a different color can make it stand out.

- **Keep It Simple**: While it's tempting to use all the formatting tools available, simplicity often works best. Overloading your worksheet with too many styles can make it look cluttered and difficult to read.

Real-World Example: Creating a Budget Spreadsheet

Let's say you're creating a budget spreadsheet for the year. Here's how you can apply cell styles and formatting to make it effective:

1. **Headers**: Start by entering headers like "Month," "Income," "Expenses," and "Balance" in the first row. Select this row and apply a bold, centered style from the Cell Styles gallery to make them stand out.

2. **Data Entries**: Enter your monthly data in the rows below. Format the "Income" and "Expenses" columns with the Currency number format to clearly show monetary values.

3. **Totals and Averages**: At the bottom, add rows for totals and averages. Use the SUM and AVERAGE functions to calculate these. Highlight these rows with a different color and bold font to differentiate them from the rest of the data.

Conditional Formatting

Conditional formatting is a powerful tool that changes the appearance of cells based on their values. This dynamic formatting helps you quickly identify trends and outliers. Here's how to use it:

1. **Select the Data Range**: Highlight the range of cells you want to apply conditional formatting to.
2. **Open Conditional Formatting**: Go to the Home tab and click on "Conditional Formatting" in the Styles group.
3. **Choose a Rule**: Select a rule type, such as "Highlight Cell Rules" or "Top/Bottom Rules." For example, to highlight expenses above a certain amount, choose "Highlight Cell Rules" > "Greater Than" and enter the threshold value.

Practical Tips for Conditional Formatting

- **Visual Cues**: Use color scales to represent data ranges visually. For instance, a gradient from green to red can indicate low to high expenses.
- **Data Bars**: These bars within cells provide a visual representation of the values, making it easy to compare at a glance.
- **Icon Sets**: Add icons like arrows or traffic lights to cells to quickly convey performance, such as an upward arrow for increasing sales.

Real-World Example: Tracking Sales Performance

Imagine you're tracking sales performance across different regions. You can use conditional formatting to quickly highlight regions that are performing well or need attention:

1. **Sales Data**: Enter sales figures for each region in a column.
2. **Apply Conditional Formatting**: Select the sales data, go to Conditional Formatting, and choose "Data Bars." This will add a bar within each cell that visually represents the sales figures.
3. **Highlight Top Performers**: Add another rule to highlight cells with sales above a certain threshold in green. This makes it easy to identify top-performing regions.

Applying cell styles and formatting in Excel is like adding the finishing touches to a masterpiece. It transforms your data from a plain grid of numbers into a structured, visually appealing, and easily understandable document. By mastering the use of cell styles, custom formatting, and conditional formatting, you can make your spreadsheets not only look professional but also enhance their functionality.

Whether you're creating a budget, tracking sales, or managing any kind of data, the right formatting techniques will help you present your information clearly and effectively. Remember, the goal of formatting is to make your data easier to read, interpret, and use. With these skills, you'll turn any spreadsheet into a powerful tool for analysis and communication. So go ahead, start experimenting with styles and formatting, and watch your data come to life.

3.2 USING CONDITIONAL FORMATTING

Imagine you've just entered a month's worth of sales data into Excel. Looking at rows and rows of numbers, it's hard to spot trends or outliers at a glance. This is where conditional formatting comes in. Conditional formatting is like a spotlight that highlights the most important data based on rules you set, making patterns and anomalies stand out. It transforms a bland spreadsheet into a dynamic tool for analysis.

Understanding Conditional Formatting

Conditional formatting changes the appearance of cells based on their values or other criteria. For instance, you can set a rule to highlight sales figures above a certain threshold in green, and those below in red. This visual differentiation helps you quickly identify high and low performers without scanning through each number.

Setting Up Conditional Formatting

Let's walk through the steps to apply conditional formatting to your data. Suppose you're tracking monthly sales figures:

1. **Select the Data Range**: Highlight the cells that contain the sales data.
2. **Open Conditional Formatting**: Go to the Home tab on the Ribbon and click on "Conditional Formatting" in the Styles group.
3. **Choose a Rule Type**: From the dropdown menu, select the type of rule you want to apply. Common options include:
   - **Highlight Cell Rules**: Highlight cells that meet certain criteria, such as being greater than a specific value.
   - **Top/Bottom Rules**: Highlight the top 10% of values or the bottom 10%, for instance.
   - **Data Bars**: Add bars to cells to create a visual representation of their values.
   - **Color Scales**: Apply a gradient of colors to show the range of values from low to high.
   - **Icon Sets**: Use icons to categorize values into different groups.

Applying a Highlight Cell Rule

Let's say you want to highlight all sales figures above $10,000 in green:

1. **Select the Sales Data**: Highlight the range of cells with your sales figures.
2. **Open Conditional Formatting**: In the Home tab, click "Conditional Formatting" > "Highlight Cell Rules" > "Greater Than".
3. **Set the Criteria**: Enter "10000" in the dialog box and choose a green fill color.
4. **Apply the Rule**: Click OK. Now, all cells with values above $10,000 will be highlighted in green.

Using Data Bars for Visual Comparison

Data bars add a horizontal bar within each cell, providing a visual representation of the value:

1. **Select the Data Range**: Highlight your sales data.
2. **Open Conditional Formatting**: Click on "Conditional Formatting" > "Data Bars".

3. **Choose a Style**: Select a color style for your data bars. Excel will automatically apply the bars, with the length corresponding to the value in each cell.

Utilizing Color Scales to Show Value Ranges

Color scales apply a gradient of colors across your data range, helping you see the distribution of values:

1. **Select the Data Range**: Highlight the sales figures.
2. **Open Conditional Formatting**: Click on "Conditional Formatting" > "Color Scales".
3. **Choose a Color Scale**: Select a color scale that ranges from one color (e.g., green for low values) to another (e.g., red for high values). Excel will apply the gradient based on the values in your data range.

Applying Icon Sets for Quick Categorization

Icon sets use symbols to categorize data into different segments, such as traffic lights or arrows:

1. **Select the Data Range**: Highlight the cells with your data.
2. **Open Conditional Formatting**: Click "Conditional Formatting" > "Icon Sets".
3. **Choose an Icon Set**: Select a set of icons that best represent the categorization you need, such as arrows for increasing/decreasing values.

Real-World Example: Monitoring Employee Performance

Imagine you're managing a team and want to monitor performance metrics like sales, customer feedback scores, and task completion rates. Here's how you can use conditional formatting to get a quick overview:

1. **Sales Figures**: Apply data bars to the sales figures to see at a glance who has the highest and lowest sales.
2. **Feedback Scores**: Use color scales to highlight customer feedback scores. A gradient from red to green can show poor to excellent feedback.
3. **Task Completion**: Apply an icon set with check marks, exclamation points, and Xs to indicate completed tasks, pending tasks, and overdue tasks, respectively.

Combining Multiple Rules

You can apply multiple conditional formatting rules to the same data range. For example, you might want to highlight sales figures above $10,000 in green, below $5,000 in red, and use data bars to show the distribution of all values. Here's how:

1. **Apply the First Rule**: Highlight cells above $10,000 in green.
2. **Apply the Second Rule**: Highlight cells below $5,000 in red.
3. **Apply Data Bars**: Add data bars to visualize the range of values.

Managing and Editing Rules

As you work with conditional formatting, you might need to adjust or remove rules. Here's how:

1. **Open Conditional Formatting Rules Manager**: Go to Home > Conditional Formatting > Manage Rules.

2. **Edit or Delete Rules**: In the Rules Manager, you can select a rule to edit it or delete it entirely. You can also change the order in which rules are applied.

Practical Tips for Effective Conditional Formatting

- **Use Sparingly**: Too many rules can make your spreadsheet look cluttered. Focus on highlighting the most important data.
- **Choose Contrasting Colors**: Ensure the colors you choose for highlighting provide clear contrast for easy readability.
- **Test Your Rules**: Apply conditional formatting to a small data set first to see how it looks before applying it to a larger range.

Conditional formatting is a powerful tool that enhances your ability to analyze and interpret data in Excel. By setting up rules to highlight, visualize, and categorize your data, you can transform a static spreadsheet into a dynamic visual aid. Whether you're tracking sales performance, monitoring employee productivity, or managing any form of data, conditional formatting helps you quickly identify trends, outliers, and key insights.

As you become more comfortable with these tools, you'll find that conditional formatting not only makes your data more attractive but also significantly more useful. It turns your Excel worksheets into actionable insights at a glance, making you more efficient and effective in your work. So go ahead, experiment with these features, and watch as your data comes to life with meaningful visual highlights.

3.3 CUSTOMIZING NUMBER FORMATS

Imagine you're working with a spreadsheet filled with numbers. These numbers could represent anything from financial data to dates to percentages. To make your data more readable and meaningful, you can customize the way these numbers are displayed. Customizing number formats in Excel allows you to control the appearance of your data without changing its actual value. It's like giving your numbers a new outfit that makes them easier to understand at a glance.

Understanding Number Formats

Number formats in Excel define how data appears in a cell. This could be simple numbers, currency, percentages, dates, or even custom formats that you create. By customizing number formats, you can make your data more readable and relevant to your audience.

Applying Basic Number Formats

To get started, let's look at how to apply some basic number formats:

1. **Select the Cells**: Highlight the cells that you want to format.
2. **Open Format Cells Dialog**: Right-click on the selected cells and choose "Format Cells," or press Ctrl+1.
3. **Choose a Category**: In the Format Cells dialog box, go to the "Number" tab. Here, you'll see various categories like General, Number, Currency, Accounting, Date, Time, Percentage, Fraction, Scientific, and Text.

Customizing Number Formats

Beyond the basic formats, Excel allows you to create custom number formats. Here's how:

1. **Open Format Cells Dialog**: Follow the steps to open the Format Cells dialog.
2. **Select Custom Category**: In the Number tab, select "Custom" at the bottom of the list.
3. **Enter a Format Code**: In the Type field, enter a custom format code.

Understanding Format Codes

Format codes are the building blocks of custom number formats. They are made up of placeholders that represent different parts of a number. Here are some common placeholders:

- **0**: Displays significant zeros. For example, the format code 000 will display the number 7 as 007.
- **#**: Displays significant digits but does not display unnecessary zeros. For example, the format code ### will display the number 7 as 7.
- **. (period)**: Defines the decimal point in the number.
- **, (comma)**: Adds a thousands separator.

Customizing Currency and Financial Data

Let's say you're working with financial data and you want to display all numbers as currency, but with a custom format that includes the currency symbol, comma separators for thousands, and two decimal places:

1. **Select the Cells**: Highlight your financial data.
2. **Open Format Cells Dialog**: Right-click and select "Format Cells."
3. **Choose Custom Category**: Go to the "Custom" category.
4. **Enter Format Code**: Type the format code "$#,##0.00" and click OK.

This format code tells Excel to display the numbers with a dollar sign, comma separators, and two decimal places. For example, the number 1234.5 will be displayed as $1,234.50.

Customizing Dates and Times

Dates and times are another area where custom formats can make a big difference. Here's an example of how to customize date formats:

1. **Select the Cells**: Highlight the cells containing dates.
2. **Open Format Cells Dialog**: Right-click and select "Format Cells."
3. **Choose Custom Category**: Go to the "Custom" category.
4. **Enter Format Code**: To display the date as "January 1, 2024," enter the format code mmmm d, yyyy and click OK.

Real-World Example: Creating an Invoice

Imagine you're creating an invoice in Excel and you want to ensure that all monetary values are formatted consistently:

1. **Set Up Your Invoice Layout**: Include headers like "Description," "Quantity," "Unit Price," and "Total."
2. **Enter Data**: Input the items, quantities, and unit prices.
3. **Calculate Totals**: Use formulas to calculate the total cost for each item and the grand total.
4. **Format Numbers**: Select all cells containing monetary values, open the Format Cells dialog, choose the "Custom" category, and enter the format code "$#,##0.00". This will ensure all prices are displayed with a dollar sign, comma separators, and two decimal places.

Advanced Custom Number Formats

You can create even more sophisticated formats by combining different placeholders and adding text. For example:

1. **Phone Numbers**: To format phone numbers like (123) 456-7890, use the format code "(###) ###-####".
2. **Percentages with Text**: To display a number as a percentage with the word "Growth" after it, use the format code 0.00% "Growth".

Practical Tips for Custom Number Formats

- **Experiment with Codes**: Don't hesitate to try different format codes to see how they affect your data.
- **Use Preview**: The Format Cells dialog shows a preview of how your data will look with the applied format.
- **Combine Formats**: You can combine multiple codes in one format. For example, "$#,##0.00;[Red]($#,##0.00)" displays positive numbers in black and negative numbers in red with parentheses.

Troubleshooting Custom Number Formats

If your custom format isn't displaying as expected, double-check the format code for errors. Ensure you're using the correct placeholders and that your data type matches the format. For instance, applying a date format to text data won't work correctly.

Customizing number formats in Excel is a powerful way to enhance the readability and professionalism of your spreadsheets. Whether you're handling financial data, dates, or specialized information, custom formats help present your data in the most meaningful way.

By mastering custom number formats, you can ensure your data is not only accurate but also easy to interpret at a glance. This skill is invaluable for creating polished, professional spreadsheets that communicate your data clearly and effectively. So, start experimenting with custom formats and watch as your Excel sheets transform into organized, visually appealing documents.

4. BASIC FORMULAS AND FUNCTIONS

Imagine opening Excel and seeing all those rows and columns stretching out before you. It might feel a bit overwhelming at first, but don't worry. The real power of Excel lies in its ability to perform calculations and automate tasks using formulas and functions. These tools transform Excel from a simple data storage tool into a dynamic powerhouse for analysis and problem-solving.

Think of formulas as the math equations you used in school, but turbocharged. They allow you to perform arithmetic operations, like addition and multiplication, directly in your spreadsheets. Functions, on the other hand, are like built-in shortcuts that make complex calculations a breeze. Instead of writing out long formulas, you can use functions to quickly find sums, averages, counts, and more.

In this chapter, we'll embark on a journey to uncover the basics of Excel formulas and functions. You'll learn how to create simple formulas to add, subtract, multiply, and divide numbers. Then, we'll dive into essential functions like SUM, AVERAGE, and COUNT, which will become your best friends in data analysis.

Imagine you're managing your household budget, tracking expenses, and income. With a few formulas and functions, you can quickly see how much you've spent, how much you've saved, and where your money is going. Or picture yourself as a small business owner analyzing monthly sales data. Functions can help you determine total sales, average sales per day, and even count the number of transactions.

By the end of this chapter, you'll feel confident creating and using basic formulas and functions. These foundational skills will open up a world of possibilities, making your work in Excel more efficient and insightful. So, let's dive in and start unlocking the true potential of your data with the magic of formulas and functions.

4.1 INTRODUCTION TO FORMULAS

Imagine you're sitting at your desk, looking at a blank Excel spreadsheet. Rows and columns stretch out before you, a grid of endless possibilities. But how do you turn these empty cells into a powerful tool for managing your data? The answer lies in mastering formulas, the core of Excel's functionality. Formulas allow you to perform calculations, automate tasks, and analyze data quickly and efficiently.

What is a Formula?

A formula in Excel is an equation that performs calculations on values in your worksheet. Formulas can be as simple as adding two numbers or as complex as calculating the interest on a loan. Every formula in Excel begins with an equals sign (=). This tells Excel that the following characters constitute a formula.

Creating Simple Formulas

Let's start with the basics: simple arithmetic operations. Imagine you have a list of expenses and you want to calculate the total. Here's how you can do it step-by-step:

1. **Enter Data**: Type your expense values into cells A1 to A5.
2. **Select a Cell for the Formula**: Click on cell A6, where you want the total to appear.
3. **Type the Formula**: Type =A1+A2+A3+A4+A5 and press Enter. Excel calculates the sum of the values in cells A1 through A5 and displays the result in cell A6.

Using Cell References

One of the strengths of Excel formulas is their ability to use cell references. Instead of hard-coding numbers, you reference the cells that contain the numbers. This makes your formulas dynamic and adaptable. For example:

- **Relative References**: These adjust when you copy the formula to another cell. If you copy the formula =A1+A2 from cell B1 to cell B2, it becomes =A2+A3.
- **Absolute References**: These remain constant, no matter where you copy the formula. Use the dollar sign ($) to create an absolute reference. For example, A1 always refers to cell A1.

Combining Functions with Formulas

Excel has a rich library of functions that you can combine with your formulas. Functions are predefined formulas that perform specific calculations. For example, the SUM function adds up a range of cells:

1. **Select the Cell**: Click on cell A6.
2. **Type the Function**: Type =SUM(A1:A5) and press Enter. Excel calculates the sum of the values in cells A1 through A5 and displays the result in cell A6.

Practical Tips for Using Formulas

- **Use Parentheses for Clarity**: Parentheses help control the order of operations in complex formulas. For example, =(A1+B1)*C1 ensures that A1 and B1 are added first, then the result is multiplied by C1.
- **Check Your Work**: Always double-check your formulas to ensure they are calculating correctly. A small error can lead to significant inaccuracies in your data analysis.
- **Keep it Simple**: Start with simple formulas and gradually build complexity as you become more comfortable. This helps you avoid errors and understand the fundamentals better.

Real-World Example: Budget Management

Let's say you're managing a household budget. You have categories like groceries, utilities, and entertainment, and you need to track your monthly spending. Here's how you can use formulas to make this task easier:

1. **Set Up Your Worksheet**: In column A, list your expense categories (Groceries, Utilities, Entertainment). In column B, enter the corresponding amounts.
2. **Calculate Total Expenses**: In cell B5, type =SUM(B1:B3) to calculate your total expenses.
3. **Compare to Budget**: If your budget is in cell B6, use a formula like =B6-B5 in cell B7 to see how much budget you have left.

Error Handling in Formulas

Excel provides tools to handle errors in formulas, ensuring your data remains accurate and meaningful. Common errors include:

- **#DIV/0!**: This error occurs when you try to divide by zero. To handle it, use the IFERROR function. For example, =IFERROR(A1/B1, "Error") returns "Error" instead of the #DIV/0! message.
- **#VALUE!**: This error happens when the formula has the wrong type of argument. Ensure all cell references and data types are correct.

Using Named Ranges

Named ranges make your formulas easier to read and manage. Instead of using cell references, you can assign names to ranges of cells. For example:

1. **Define a Named Range**: Select the cells A1 to A5, then click on the Name Box (next to the formula bar) and type "Expenses."
2. **Use Named Range in Formulas**: In cell A6, type =SUM(Expenses) and press Enter. Excel calculates the sum of the named range.

Mastering formulas in Excel transforms how you handle data, turning a simple grid into a powerful tool for analysis and decision-making. By understanding the basics of creating and using formulas, you can automate calculations, reduce errors, and gain deeper insights from your data.

Whether you're tracking a budget, analyzing sales figures, or managing project timelines, formulas are the foundation that makes Excel an indispensable part of your toolkit. So take your time, experiment with different formulas, and watch as your data comes to life in new and meaningful ways. With practice, you'll find that creating and using formulas becomes second nature, empowering you to tackle any data challenge with confidence.

4.2 ESSENTIAL FUNCTIONS (SUM, AVERAGE, COUNT)

Imagine you're sitting down with a cup of coffee, ready to tackle your monthly expenses in Excel. You have a list of transactions, and you want to understand your spending habits. This is where Excel's essential functions come into play, transforming raw data into meaningful insights with just a few simple commands. Among these, SUM, AVERAGE, and COUNT are your go-to tools, each serving a unique purpose in analyzing your data.

The SUM Function: Adding It All Up

The SUM function is like your trusty calculator, adding up numbers across a range of cells effortlessly. Let's say you have a column of expenses and you want to find the total amount spent.

1. **Enter Your Data**: In column A, list your expenses from A1 to A10.
2. **Select the Cell for the Total**: Click on cell A11, where you want the total to appear.
3. **Type the SUM Function**: Type =SUM(A1:A10) and press Enter.

Excel will instantly calculate the total of the values in cells A1 through A10. This function is incredibly useful for budgeting, financial analysis, and any scenario where you need to add up a series of numbers.

Practical Tips for Using SUM

- **Using AutoSum**: For a quick sum, select the cell below your column of numbers and click the AutoSum button on the Home tab. Excel will automatically generate the SUM function for the adjacent range.
- **Summing Multiple Ranges**: You can sum multiple ranges at once. For example, =SUM(A1:A5, B1:B5) adds up both ranges.

Real-World Example: Summing Daily Sales

Imagine you're tracking daily sales for your small business. You enter each day's sales in column B. At the end of the month, use the SUM function in cell B31 to calculate the total monthly sales with =SUM(B1:B30). This provides a quick overview of your monthly performance.

The AVERAGE Function: Finding the Middle Ground

The AVERAGE function calculates the mean of a group of numbers, giving you an idea of the typical value in your data set. Suppose you want to find the average amount spent on groceries over the past month.

1. **Enter Your Data**: List your grocery expenses in column B from B1 to B10.
2. **Select the Cell for the Average**: Click on cell B11.
3. **Type the AVERAGE Function**: Type =AVERAGE(B1:B10) and press Enter.

Excel will calculate the average of the values in cells B1 through B10. This function is particularly useful for analyzing data trends, such as average sales, grades, or temperatures.

Practical Tips for Using AVERAGE

- **Ignoring Zero Values**: If you want to calculate the average without including zeros, use the AVERAGEIF function: =AVERAGEIF(B1:B10, "<>0").
- **Handling Non-Numeric Data**: Ensure all cells in the range contain numeric data. Text or errors in the range will cause the AVERAGE function to return an error.

Real-World Example: Analyzing Employee Performance

Imagine you're a manager evaluating employee performance scores. Enter each employee's score in column C. Use the AVERAGE function in cell C11 to calculate the average performance score with =AVERAGE(C1:C10). This helps you understand the overall performance level in your team.

The COUNT Function: Counting Entries

The COUNT function counts the number of cells that contain numeric data in a range. It's useful for understanding the quantity of entries in a dataset, such as the number of transactions or items sold.

1. **Enter Your Data**: List your items sold in column D from D1 to D10.
2. **Select the Cell for the Count**: Click on cell D11.
3. **Type the COUNT Function**: Type =COUNT(D1:D10) and press Enter.

Excel will count the number of numeric entries in the specified range. This function is helpful for inventory management, attendance tracking, and any scenario where you need to count occurrences.

Practical Tips for Using COUNT

- **Counting All Data Types**: If you want to count all non-empty cells, use the COUNTA function instead: =COUNTA(D1:D10).
- **Handling Errors**: The COUNT function only counts cells with numbers. Ensure your data range is free from text or error values if you want an accurate count of numbers.

Real-World Example: Inventory Tracking

Suppose you're managing a warehouse and need to count the number of different products in stock. Enter each product's quantity in column E. Use the COUNT function in cell E11 with =COUNT(E1:E10) to find out how many products have recorded quantities.

Combining Functions for Enhanced Analysis

Excel's true power shines when you combine these functions to perform more complex analyses. For instance, you might want to calculate the average sales only for days with sales above a certain amount. You can achieve this by combining AVERAGE and IF functions, like so:

1. **Conditional Average**: Use =AVERAGEIF(B1:B30, ">100") to find the average sales for days where sales were greater than $100.

This combination allows for deeper insights and more nuanced data analysis, making Excel an incredibly versatile tool.

Mastering the SUM, AVERAGE, and COUNT functions in Excel is a crucial step in transforming how you handle data. These essential functions provide quick, reliable methods for performing fundamental calculations, making your data analysis more efficient and insightful.

Whether you're managing a budget, tracking sales, analyzing performance, or handling inventory, these functions will be your best friends. Practice using them in different contexts, and you'll soon find that you can glean meaningful insights from your data with ease. With these tools at your disposal, you're well on your way to becoming an Excel expert, ready to tackle any data challenge with confidence. So go ahead, dive into your data, and watch as these essential functions make your life easier and your work more impactful.

4.3 USING CELL REFERENCES (RELATIVE, ABSOLUTE, MIXED)

Imagine you're working on a budget spreadsheet in Excel, and you want to calculate the total expenses for each month. You start by entering your data and creating a simple formula to sum up the expenses for January. But what happens when you want to copy that formula to calculate totals for the other months? This is where understanding cell references—relative, absolute, and mixed—becomes crucial. These concepts help ensure that your formulas work correctly across your entire worksheet, making your tasks much easier and more efficient.

Relative Cell References

Relative cell references change based on their relative position to the cell in which the formula is copied. These are the most commonly used references in Excel and are perfect for scenarios where you want the same calculation applied across multiple rows or columns.

Example: Copying a Simple Sum Formula

1. **Enter Your Data**: In column A, list your expenses for January (A1 to A5). In column B, list your expenses for February (B1 to B5).
2. **Create a Formula**: In cell A6, enter the formula =SUM(A1:A5) to calculate the total expenses for January.
3. **Copy the Formula**: Click on cell A6, then drag the fill handle (a small square at the bottom-right corner of the cell) across to cell B6. The formula =SUM(A1:A5) will automatically adjust to =SUM(B1:B5).

Absolute Cell References

Absolute cell references do not change when you copy the formula to another cell. These references are fixed and are useful when you want to refer to a specific cell, regardless of where the formula is copied. Absolute references are denoted by dollar signs ($) before the column letter and row number.

Example: Using a Constant Value in a Calculation

1. **Enter a Constant Value**: In cell D1, enter the tax rate (e.g., 0.08 for 8%).
2. **Calculate Total with Tax**: In cell A7, enter the formula =A6*(1+D1) to calculate the total expenses for January including tax.
3. **Copy the Formula**: Drag the fill handle from cell A7 across to cell B7. The formula will adjust the relative references for each month but will keep the tax rate reference fixed as D1.

Mixed Cell References

Mixed cell references are a combination of relative and absolute references. These references lock either the row or the column but not both. Mixed references are useful when you need part of your formula to adjust as you copy it to other cells while keeping another part constant.

Example: Applying a Formula Across Rows and Columns

1. **Enter Data**: In column A, list different products. In row 1, list the sales months.
2. **Enter Unit Prices and Quantities**: In cell B2, enter the unit price of the first product. In cell C2, enter the quantity sold in January.
3. **Create a Mixed Reference Formula**: In cell D2, enter the formula =$B2*C$1 to calculate total sales. Here, $B2 locks the column B (unit price), and C$1 locks row 1 (quantity sold).
4. **Copy the Formula**: Drag the fill handle from cell D2 across the rows and columns. The formula will adjust relative references for the quantities sold but will keep the unit price and the month constant where needed.

Practical Tips for Using Cell References

- **Consistency in Formulas**: Use relative references when you need the formula to adjust to different cells. Use absolute references when you need to lock a specific cell or value.
- **Easier Copying**: By understanding and using the right type of cell reference, you save time and reduce errors when copying formulas across multiple cells.
- **Combining References**: Don't hesitate to mix relative, absolute, and mixed references within the same formula to get the desired outcome.

Real-World Example: Calculating Discounts

Imagine you're managing a sales sheet where you need to apply a discount to different products:

1. **Enter Original Prices**: List the original prices of products in column A (A1 to A10).
2. **Enter Discount Rate**: In cell B1, enter the discount rate (e.g., 0.10 for 10%).
3. **Calculate Discounted Prices**: In cell B2, enter the formula =A2*(1-B1) to apply the discount to the first product.
4. **Copy the Formula**: Drag the fill handle from cell B2 down to B10. The formula will adjust the relative reference for each product price while keeping the discount rate fixed.

Error Handling and Best Practices

- **Double-Check References**: When copying formulas, always double-check that the cell references adjust correctly. Incorrect references can lead to errors or inaccurate calculations.
- **Use F4 for Quick Absolute References**: While typing a formula, pressing F4 after selecting a cell reference will cycle through the different types of references (relative, absolute, mixed).
- **Organize Your Data**: Keep constant values (like tax rates or discount percentages) in separate cells and use absolute references to refer to them. This makes it easy to update these values without changing multiple formulas.

Understanding and using cell references—relative, absolute, and mixed—is essential for creating accurate and efficient formulas in Excel. These references allow you to manipulate and analyze data dynamically, ensuring your calculations are flexible and robust.

Whether you're managing budgets, analyzing sales, or calculating discounts, mastering cell references will make your work in Excel more powerful and precise. Practice using these references in different scenarios, and you'll soon find that you can handle any data challenge with ease. So, go ahead, experiment with cell references, and watch as your Excel skills grow and your spreadsheets become more effective and insightful.

5. DATA ORGANIZATION AND MANAGEMENT

Imagine walking into a room filled with stacks of papers, each pile representing critical data for your business. Without a clear organization system, finding a specific piece of information would be a nightmare. This is where Excel's data organization and management features come to the rescue, transforming chaotic data into structured, accessible, and meaningful information.

In today's data-driven world, efficiently managing and organizing data is essential. Whether you're handling customer records, inventory lists, or financial reports, Excel offers robust tools to help you keep your data orderly and easy to navigate. By mastering these features, you can ensure that your data is not only well-organized but also readily available for analysis and decision-making.

Think of Excel as your digital filing cabinet, equipped with advanced functionalities to sort, filter, and validate data, making it simpler to manage large datasets. Proper data organization is the backbone of effective data analysis, enabling you to uncover trends, make informed decisions, and present your findings clearly.

This chapter will guide you through the essential techniques for organizing and managing data in Excel. We'll explore how to sort and filter data to find what you need quickly, use tables to manage large datasets efficiently, and implement data validation to ensure the accuracy and consistency of your entries. These tools and techniques will empower you to handle your data with confidence and precision.

As we delve into these topics, remember that the goal is not just to clean up your spreadsheet but to create a system where data flows seamlessly, allowing you to focus on extracting valuable insights. So, let's embark on this journey to master Excel's data organization and management features, turning your spreadsheets into powerful tools for business intelligence and decision-making.

5.1 SORTING AND FILTERING DATA

Imagine you're in a library with thousands of books scattered randomly on the shelves. Finding the book you need would be an overwhelming task. Now, think of your Excel spreadsheet as that library. Sorting and filtering your data is akin to organizing those books systematically, making it easier to find exactly what you're looking for. This chapter will guide you through the process of sorting and filtering data in Excel 2024, ensuring your data is not only accessible but also meaningful.

Sorting Data: Bringing Order to Chaos

Sorting data in Excel allows you to arrange your information in a specific order, making it easier to analyze and understand. Whether you want to sort alphabetically, numerically, or by date, Excel provides powerful sorting options to meet your needs.

Step-by-Step Guide to Sorting Data

1. **Select the Data Range:**
   - Highlight the range of cells you want to sort. This can include the entire table or just a specific column.

2. **Access the Sort Feature:**
   - Go to the Data tab on the ribbon. Click on Sort to open the Sort dialog box.

3. **Choose Sorting Criteria:**
   - In the Sort dialog box, select the column by which you want to sort your data. Choose the sort order (ascending or descending). For example, to sort names alphabetically, select the column containing the names and choose ascending order.

4. **Add Levels (if needed):**
   - If you need to sort by multiple criteria (e.g., first by department, then by employee name), click Add Level and specify the additional sorting criteria.

5. **Apply the Sort:**
   - Click OK to apply the sort. Your data will be rearranged according to the specified criteria.

Practical Tips for Sorting Data

- **Header Row:** Ensure your data has a header row. Excel typically recognizes headers and excludes them from the sort.
- **Check for Merged Cells:** Unmerge any merged cells within the range to avoid sorting issues.
- **Custom Lists:** Use custom lists for sorting non-standard sequences (e.g., sorting days of the week starting with Monday).

Real-World Example: Sorting Sales Data

Imagine you have a spreadsheet with sales data including columns for the date, sales representative, product, and sales amount. To analyze the performance of your sales team, you want to sort the data by sales amount in descending order.

1. **Select the Range:**
   - Highlight the entire table.

2. **Open the Sort Dialog:**
   - Go to Data > Sort.

3. **Sort by Sales Amount:**
   - Select the column containing sales amounts and choose descending order.

4. **Review the Sorted Data:**
   - Your table now displays the highest sales amounts at the top, making it easier to identify top performers.

Filtering Data: Zeroing In on What Matters

Filtering allows you to display only the rows that meet certain criteria, effectively hiding the rest. This is particularly useful for large datasets where you need to focus on specific information without being distracted by irrelevant data.

Step-by-Step Guide to Filtering Data

1. **Select the Data Range:**
   o Click anywhere within the data range you want to filter.
2. **Enable Filtering:**
   o Go to the Data tab and click on Filter. Small dropdown arrows will appear in the header row of each column.
3. **Apply a Filter:**
   o Click the dropdown arrow in the column header you want to filter. A list of filter options will appear.
   o Choose the criteria for your filter. For example, to view sales by a specific representative, select the representative's name from the list.
4. **View Filtered Data:**
   o The spreadsheet will now display only the rows that meet your filter criteria.

Practical Tips for Filtering Data

- **Multiple Filters:** You can apply filters to multiple columns simultaneously for more precise data analysis.
- **Clear Filters:** To remove a filter, click the filter icon in the column header and select Clear Filter from [Column Name].
- **Text Filters:** Use text filters for columns containing text to include options like "contains" or "begins with".

Real-World Example: Filtering Customer Feedback

Suppose you have a dataset with customer feedback, including columns for customer name, feedback date, product, and comments. You want to view feedback for a specific product.

1. **Enable Filtering:**
   o Click anywhere in your data range and go to Data > Filter.
2. **Filter by Product:**
   o Click the filter arrow in the product column header, and select the specific product you're interested in.
3. **Analyze Feedback:**
   o The spreadsheet now displays only the feedback related to the selected product, making it easier to analyze customer opinions.

Combining Sorting and Filtering for Maximum Efficiency

Sorting and filtering can be used together to refine your data further. For example, you might sort your sales data by date and then filter it to show only the entries for a specific sales representative.

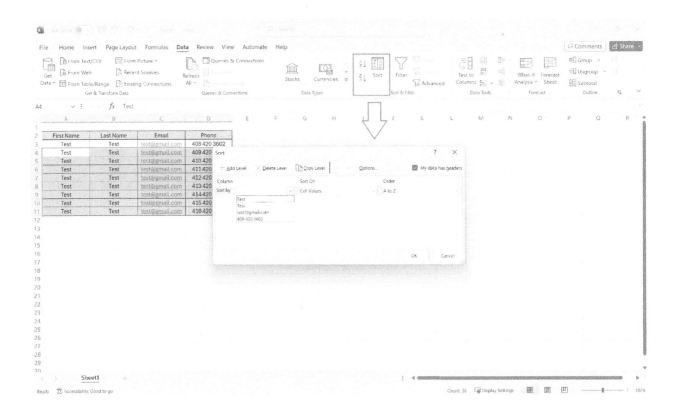

Real-World Example: Analyzing Monthly Sales for Top Performer

1. **Sort by Date:**
   o   Highlight your sales data and sort it by date in ascending order.

2. **Filter by Sales Representative:**
   o   Apply a filter to display data only for your top-performing sales representative.

3. **Review Sorted and Filtered Data:**
   o   You now have a chronological view of all sales made by your top performer, allowing for detailed analysis.

Sorting and filtering are fundamental tools in Excel that transform your ability to manage and analyze data. By mastering these techniques, you can organize large datasets efficiently, pinpoint relevant information quickly, and derive meaningful insights with ease. Remember, the goal is to create a clear, organized system that makes your data work for you, rather than overwhelming you. With these skills, you'll be well-equipped to handle any data organization challenge that comes your way, ensuring your spreadsheets are both functional and insightful.

5.2 USING TABLES FOR DATA MANAGEMENT

Imagine your data as a sprawling garden. Without organization, it can quickly become a tangled mess. Using tables in Excel is like laying out neat rows and pathways, making every part of your garden accessible and manageable. Tables transform raw data into structured, dynamic sets that are easy to analyze and update. This chapter will guide you through the process of using tables for data management, ensuring your data is both organized and powerful.

Why Use Tables in Excel?

Tables in Excel offer several advantages over simple ranges of data. They automatically expand as you add new data, maintain consistent formatting, and provide built-in sorting and filtering capabilities. These features make tables an essential tool for managing large datasets efficiently.

Creating a Table: A Step-by-Step Guide

1. **Select Your Data Range:**
   o   Highlight the range of cells that you want to convert into a table. Ensure your range includes column headers.

2. **Insert a Table:**
   o   Go to the Insert tab on the ribbon and click on Table. Excel will prompt you to confirm the range and whether your table has headers.

3. **Confirm Table Creation:**
   o   Click OK to create the table. Excel will format your data as a table, adding filter buttons to each column header.

Customizing Your Table

Once your table is created, you can customize it to better suit your needs.

1. **Rename the Table:**
   o   Click on any cell within the table, go to the Table Design tab, and enter a new name in the Table Name box. A descriptive name helps you identify the table easily in formulas.

2. **Change the Table Style:**
   o   In the Table Design tab, select a style from the Table Styles gallery. This allows you to apply different color schemes and formatting options.

3. **Add Total Row:**
    o   To add a total row at the bottom of your table, check the Total Row box in the Table Design tab. You can customize each cell in this row to perform different calculations, such as SUM, AVERAGE, or COUNT.

Practical Tips for Table Customization

*   **Alternate Row Colors:** Use alternate row colors to improve readability.
*   **Freeze Headers:** Freeze the top row to keep column headers visible as you scroll.
*   **Custom Formulas:** Use structured references in formulas for clarity and efficiency.

Using Table Features for Data Management

Tables come with powerful features that enhance data management, such as sorting, filtering, and dynamic updates.

1. **Sorting Data:**
    o   Click the filter arrow in the column header and select Sort A to Z or Sort Z to A to sort your data alphabetically or numerically. For custom sorts, select Sort by Color or Sort by Custom List.
2. **Filtering Data:**
    o   Use the filter arrows to display only the rows that meet certain criteria. For example, you can filter sales data to show only transactions above a certain amount.
3. **Adding Data:**
    o   Simply type in the row immediately below the table, and it will automatically expand to include the new data. This dynamic range ensures your table always encompasses all your data.

Real-World Example: Managing Employee Records

Imagine you manage a company's HR data, including employee names, departments, hire dates, and salaries. Here's how you can organize this data using tables:

1. **Create the Table:**
    o   Select the range of your employee data and insert a table.
2. **Customize the Table:**
    o   Rename the table to EmployeeData. Apply a style that uses alternate row colors for better readability.
3. **Sort and Filter:**
    o   Sort employees by hire date to see who has been with the company the longest. Filter by department to focus on specific teams.
4. **Add Data:**
    o   As new employees join, simply add their details in the next available row. The table will automatically include the new entries.

Advanced Table Features

Excel tables also support more advanced features, such as creating pivot tables, using slicers for visual filtering, and leveraging structured references in formulas.

1. **Creating PivotTables:**
   - Select any cell within the table, go to the Insert tab, and click PivotTable. Choose where to place the PivotTable and click OK. You can now analyze your data dynamically.

2. **Using Slicers:**
   - To add slicers for quick filtering, go to the Table Design tab and click Insert Slicer. Select the columns for which you want to create slicers. This feature provides a visual way to filter data.

3. **Structured References:**
   - Use structured references in formulas to make your calculations clearer and more reliable. For example, to sum the salary column, use:

   =SUM(EmployeeData[Salary])

Practical Tips for Advanced Features

- **Regular Updates:** Regularly update your tables with new data to keep your analysis current.
- **Consistent Naming:** Use consistent and descriptive names for tables and columns to make formulas and references more understandable.
- **Explore PivotTables:** Take advantage of PivotTables to summarize and analyze large datasets quickly.

Real-World Example: Tracking Sales Performance

Suppose you're tracking sales data across different regions and products. Here's how to leverage advanced table features:

1. **Create a Sales Table:**
   - Insert a table for your sales data and name it SalesData.

2. **Add Slicers:**
   - Insert slicers for regions and products to filter sales performance visually.

3. **Generate a PivotTable:**
   - Create a PivotTable to analyze total sales by region and product category. Use structured references to ensure accurate calculations.

Using tables in Excel is a transformative approach to data management. Tables not only organize your data but also enhance its functionality, making it easier to sort, filter, and analyze information efficiently. By mastering tables, you can ensure your data remains structured and dynamic, ready to support insightful analysis and decision-making. Embrace these powerful features to elevate your Excel skills and handle your data with confidence and precision.

5.3 DATA VALIDATION TECHNIQUES

Imagine you're running a gourmet restaurant, and you want to ensure that every ingredient that goes into your dishes meets the highest standards. In the world of Excel, data validation is like your quality control, ensuring that the information entered into your spreadsheets is accurate, consistent, and reliable. This chapter will guide you through the essential data validation techniques, helping you maintain the integrity of your data and prevent errors before they occur.

What is Data Validation?

Data validation is a feature in Excel that allows you to define rules for what data can be entered into a cell. By setting these rules, you can control the type, range, and format of data, thereby reducing errors and ensuring consistency. This is particularly useful when multiple users are entering data into the same workbook.

Setting Up Data Validation: Step-by-Step Guide

1. **Select the Cell or Range:**
   o   Highlight the cell or range of cells where you want to apply data validation.
2. **Access Data Validation:**
   o   Go to the Data tab on the ribbon and click on Data Validation in the Data Tools group.
3. **Define Validation Criteria:**
   o   In the Data Validation dialog box, go to the Settings tab.
   o   From the Allow dropdown menu, choose the type of data you want to allow (e.g., Whole Number, Decimal, List, Date, Time, Text Length, or Custom).
4. **Set Specific Criteria:**
   o   Based on your selection, set the specific criteria for the data. For example, if you choose Whole Number, you can specify a range (e.g., between 1 and 100).
5. **Add Input Message (Optional):**
   o   Go to the Input Message tab to provide a message that will appear when the cell is selected. This helps users understand what type of data is expected.
6. **Set Error Alert:**
   o   On the Error Alert tab, define the message that will appear if invalid data is entered. You can choose from Stop, Warning, or Information alerts.
7. **Apply the Validation:**
   o   Click OK to apply the data validation rules to the selected cells.

Practical Tips for Data Validation

- **Use Named Ranges:** For list validation, use named ranges to make your data validation rules easier to manage and update.
- **Combine Rules:** Use the Custom option to combine multiple validation rules with formulas.
- **Regular Updates:** Regularly update your validation rules as your data requirements change.

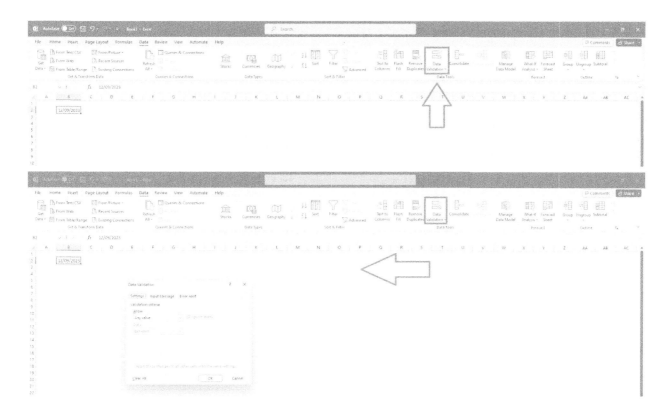

Real-World Example: Validating Employee IDs

Imagine you need to ensure that employee IDs entered into a spreadsheet are exactly five digits long. Here's how you can set up data validation to enforce this rule:

1. **Select the Range:**
   - Highlight the column where employee IDs will be entered.
2. **Access Data Validation:**
   - Go to Data > Data Validation.
3. **Set Validation Criteria:**
   - In the Data Validation dialog box, choose Text Length from the Allow dropdown menu.
   - Set the criteria to Equal to and specify 5 as the length.
4. **Add Input Message and Error Alert:**
   - Provide an input message such as "Enter a 5-digit Employee ID."
   - Set an error alert message like "Employee ID must be exactly 5 digits long."

Advanced Data Validation Techniques

Beyond basic validation rules, Excel offers advanced techniques for more complex data requirements.

Using Custom Formulas for Validation

1. **Select the Range:**
   o Highlight the cells where you want to apply the validation.
2. **Access Data Validation:**
   o Go to Data > Data Validation.
3. **Set Custom Criteria:**
   o In the Settings tab, choose Custom from the Allow dropdown menu.
   o Enter a formula to define the validation rule. For example, to ensure a date is in the current year: =YEAR(A1)=YEAR(TODAY())
4. **Apply the Validation:**
   o Click OK to apply the rule.

Dependent Drop-Down Lists

Creating dependent drop-down lists allows one list's options to change based on the selection in another list.

1. **Create Lists:**
   o Define the primary list (e.g., Categories) and secondary lists (e.g., Items within each Category).
2. **Name Ranges:**
   o Name each range corresponding to the primary list items.
3. **Set Primary List Validation:**
   o Select the cell for the primary list, go to Data Validation, and set the validation type to List, referencing the primary list range.
4. **Set Dependent List Validation:**
   o For the dependent list, use the INDIRECT function in the data validation criteria: =INDIRECT(A1)
   o This ensures that the dependent list updates based on the selection in the primary list.

Practical Tips for Advanced Techniques

- **Test Thoroughly:** Always test your validation rules to ensure they work as expected and handle edge cases.
- **User Guidance:** Use input messages and error alerts to guide users and provide clear instructions.

Real-World Example: Dependent Drop-Down Lists for Product Selection

Suppose you're managing inventory and need to create a system where selecting a product category dynamically updates the product list.

1. **Define Ranges:**
    o   Create named ranges for each product category (e.g., Fruits, Vegetables).

2. **Primary List Validation:**
    o   Apply data validation to the category cell to choose from the list of categories.

3. **Dependent List Validation:**
    o   Use the INDIRECT function in the product cell's data validation to reference the selected category's range.

Data validation in Excel is a powerful tool that ensures the accuracy and consistency of your data. By mastering these techniques, you can prevent errors before they happen, maintain the integrity of your datasets, and create a more reliable and efficient workflow. Whether you're enforcing simple rules or implementing complex validation systems, these tools will help you keep your data clean and your processes smooth. Embrace data validation to enhance your data management capabilities and ensure that your Excel spreadsheets are both robust and reliable.

6. VISUALIZING DATA WITH CHARTS

Visualizing data with charts transforms raw numbers into compelling stories. Imagine trying to explain a complex dataset to a colleague without a visual aid; it's like describing a beautiful landscape without a photograph. Charts are those photographs—they provide clarity, highlight trends, and make data digestible at a glance.

When you create charts in Excel, you're not just plotting points on a graph; you're crafting a narrative. Think of your data as a story waiting to be told. A well-designed chart can reveal the peaks and valleys, the dramatic turns, and the subtle nuances that numbers alone might obscure. For instance, a sales report bursting with figures might be daunting, but a simple line chart can instantly show whether your sales are soaring or sliding.

Excel makes this process remarkably intuitive. With a few clicks, you can transform a basic spreadsheet into a visual masterpiece. The magic begins with selecting the right type of chart for your data. Are you comparing categories? A bar chart could be your best friend. Tracking changes over time? A line chart will effortlessly convey the trend. Want to show proportions? A pie chart slices your data into digestible pieces.

Creating these charts is straightforward. Start by highlighting your data, then head to the Insert tab and choose from Excel's array of chart options. This is where your creative side gets to play. Adjust colors, labels, and titles to ensure your chart isn't just informative but also visually appealing. Remember, a clear and attractive chart is far more likely to grab and hold your audience's attention.

But it's not just about aesthetics. Customizing your charts can also enhance their functionality. Adding data labels, trendlines, or secondary axes can provide deeper insights. For example, a trendline in a sales chart can help you project future performance, offering valuable foresight based on past trends.

Excel's chart tools empower you to turn data into visuals that speak volumes. Whether you're presenting to a boardroom full of executives or explaining findings to a small team, a well-crafted chart can bridge the gap between raw data and meaningful insights. So, dive into Excel's charting features and start visualizing your data in ways that enlighten and engage.

6.1 CREATING BASIC CHARTS

Creating a basic chart in Excel is akin to turning a blank canvas into a visual story that makes data easily understandable and engaging. Let's dive into the process, step-by-step, to transform your data into clear, informative charts.

Understanding the Basics

Before jumping into chart creation, it's essential to grasp the foundational elements. Charts in Excel are visual representations of data that help highlight trends, patterns, and relationships. There are several types of charts, each suited to different kinds of data. The most commonly used are column, line, pie, bar, area, and scatter charts. Each has its unique strengths:

- **Column and Bar Charts:** Ideal for comparing different categories.
- **Line Charts:** Perfect for showing trends over time.
- **Pie Charts:** Best for illustrating proportions.
- **Scatter Charts:** Great for displaying relationships between two variables.

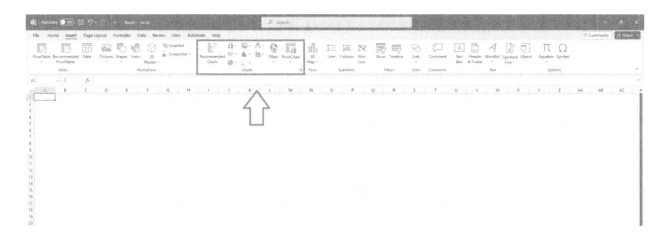

Step-by-Step Guide to Creating a Basic Chart

Let's walk through the process of creating a simple column chart to visualize data.

Step 1: Prepare Your Data

Ensure your data is well-organized. For a basic column chart, you should have your categories in one column and corresponding values in another. For instance, imagine you have sales data for the first quarter:

Month	Sales
January	1000
February	1500
March	1200

Step 2: Select Your Data

Highlight the data you want to include in your chart. Click and drag to select the range of cells. In our example, you would highlight cells A1.

Step 3: Insert the Chart

Navigate to the Insert tab on the Excel ribbon. Here, you'll find a variety of chart options. For a column chart, click on the Column or Bar Chart icon. Excel will present you with different styles, such as clustered column, stacked column, and more. For now, select the Clustered Column option.

Step 4: Customize the Chart

Once your chart appears, it's time to make it your own. Click on the chart to activate the Chart Tools tabs: Design and Format. Here's how you can customize your chart:

- **Chart Title:** Click on the chart title to edit it. Give it a descriptive name like "Q1 Sales Performance."
- **Axes Titles:** To add titles to the axes, go to the Design tab, click on Add Chart Element, then Axes Titles, and choose titles for both horizontal and vertical axes. Label them accordingly, such as "Month" and "Sales."
- **Data Labels:** Adding data labels can make your chart easier to read. In the Design tab, click on Add Chart Element, then Data Labels, and choose a position that works best for your chart.

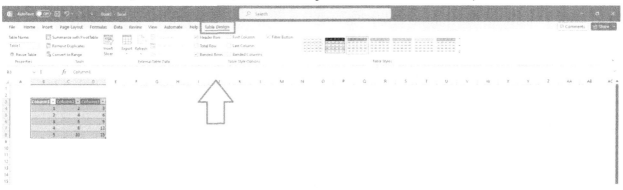

Step 5: Format the Chart

Formatting enhances the visual appeal and clarity of your chart. Here's how you can refine it:

- **Change Colors:** In the Design tab, click on Change Colors to select a color scheme that matches your preferences or presentation needs.
- **Adjusting Elements:** You can resize and reposition chart elements for better readability. Click on any element (like the legend or the chart area) and drag it to a new position or adjust its size using the handles.
- **Gridlines and Background:** You can add or remove gridlines for a cleaner look. In the Design tab, under Add Chart Element, you can toggle primary and secondary gridlines. Additionally, you can format the background by right-clicking on the chart area and selecting Format Chart Area.

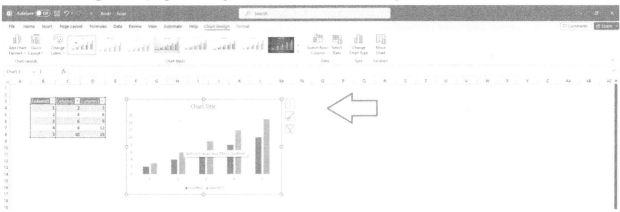

Step 6: Save Your Chart

Don't forget to save your work. Charts are saved within the Excel workbook, so ensure you save your file after making significant changes. Click File > Save As and choose your preferred location and file format.

Practical Tips for Effective Charts

Creating a chart is more than just plotting data points. It's about communicating information effectively. Here are some tips to keep in mind:

- **Keep It Simple:** Avoid clutter by including only the necessary elements. Too much information can overwhelm the viewer.
- **Be Consistent:** Use consistent colors and styles for similar data points to avoid confusion.
- **Highlight Key Data:** Use colors or labels to emphasize important data points or trends.
- **Consider Your Audience:** Tailor the complexity and detail of your chart to your audience's familiarity with the data.

Real-World Example: Monthly Expenses Chart

To bring this all together, let's create a real-world example. Suppose you want to visualize your monthly expenses to better understand your spending habits. Here's how you can do it:

1. **Prepare Your Data:** List categories and amounts.

Category	Amount
Rent	1200
Utilities	300
Groceries	450
Entertainment	150
Transportation	200

2. **Select Your Data:** Highlight the data range A1.
3. **Insert the Chart:** Go to Insert > Column or Bar Chart > Clustered Column.
4. **Customize the Chart:**
   - Title: "Monthly Expenses"
   - Axes Titles: "Category" and "Amount"
   - Data Labels: Positioned above each column.
5. **Format the Chart:** Adjust colors to differentiate categories, remove unnecessary gridlines, and resize the chart for better presentation.

By following these steps, you'll create a clear and visually appealing chart that shows where your money is going each month. This practical application helps you track expenses and identify areas where you can save, making your data not just informative but actionable.

Mastering the creation of basic charts in Excel opens up a new world of data visualization. It empowers you to present your data clearly and effectively, transforming raw numbers into meaningful stories. Whether you're tracking personal expenses, analyzing sales data, or presenting business performance, charts are invaluable tools. Practice these steps, experiment with different types of charts, and soon you'll be able to turn any dataset into an insightful visual narrative.

6.2 CUSTOMIZING CHART ELEMENTS

Customizing chart elements in Excel allows you to take a basic chart and transform it into a powerful, clear, and visually appealing representation of your data. By tailoring the various components of your chart, you can highlight key insights, make the data more accessible to your audience, and ensure your visualizations align with your specific needs and preferences. Let's explore how to customize these elements step-by-step.

Understanding Chart Elements

Before we dive into the customization process, it's essential to know the key elements of a chart. These typically include:

- **Chart Title:** The main heading that describes the chart's content.
- **Axis Titles:** Labels for the horizontal (X-axis) and vertical (Y-axis) axes.
- **Legend:** Explains the colors, symbols, or patterns used in the chart.
- **Data Labels:** Values displayed on the chart to show precise data points.
- **Gridlines:** Horizontal and vertical lines that help to measure and compare data.
- **Chart Area:** The entire chart, including all its elements.
- **Plot Area:** The area within the axes where the data is plotted.

Step-by-Step Customization

Step 1: Adding and Editing the Chart Title

A clear, descriptive title is crucial as it immediately informs the viewer about the chart's subject.

1. **Click on the Chart:** Select the chart you want to customize.
2. **Activate the Chart Title:** Click on the existing title or go to the Chart Tools ribbon, then click Add Chart Element > Chart Title.
3. **Edit the Title:** Click inside the title box and type a new title that accurately describes the data. For example, "Annual Sales Growth 2024."

Step 2: Customizing Axis Titles

Axis titles provide context, making it easier for viewers to understand what the data represents.

1. **Select the Chart:** Click on the chart to activate it.
2. **Add Axis Titles:** Go to the Chart Tools ribbon, click Add Chart Element > Axis Titles and choose between Primary Horizontal and Primary Vertical.
3. **Edit the Axis Titles:** Click on each axis title box and type in descriptive labels. For example, "Months" for the X-axis and "Sales in USD" for the Y-axis.

Step 3: Adjusting the Legend

The legend is crucial for understanding what each color or pattern represents, especially in charts with multiple data series.

1. **Select the Chart:** Click on the chart.
2. **Modify the Legend:** Go to the Chart Tools ribbon, click Add Chart Element > Legend, and choose a position such as Top, Bottom, Right, or Left.
3. **Edit Legend Entries:** If needed, click on the legend entries to change their names directly from the data source.

Step 4: Adding Data Labels

Data labels provide precise information for individual data points, making the chart easier to read.

1. **Select the Chart:** Click on the chart.
2. **Add Data Labels:** Go to the Chart Tools ribbon, click Add Chart Element > Data Labels, and choose a position such as Center, Inside End, or Outside End.
3. **Customize Data Labels:** Click on a data label to format it. You can change the font, size, and color to enhance readability.

Step 5: Configuring Gridlines

Gridlines help in comparing data points but can sometimes clutter the chart. Adjusting them appropriately enhances clarity.

1. **Select the Chart:** Click on the chart.
2. **Modify Gridlines:** Go to the Chart Tools ribbon, click Add Chart Element > Gridlines, and choose to add or remove Primary Major Horizontal, Primary Minor Horizontal, Primary Major Vertical, and Primary Minor Vertical gridlines.
3. **Format Gridlines:** Right-click on the gridlines and select Format Gridlines to change their color, style, or width.

Step 6: Formatting the Chart and Plot Area

The overall appearance of the chart can be enhanced by customizing the chart and plot areas.

1. **Select the Chart:** Click on the chart to bring up the Chart Tools ribbon.
2. **Format Chart Area:** Right-click on the chart area and choose Format Chart Area. Here you can change the fill color, border color, and effects like shadow or 3D formatting.
3. **Format Plot Area:** Right-click on the plot area and choose Format Plot Area. Similar to the chart area, you can adjust the fill, border, and effects.

Practical Tips for Effective Customization

Customizing your charts effectively requires attention to detail and a clear understanding of your audience. Here are some practical tips to keep in mind:

- **Consistency:** Use consistent colors and styles across multiple charts to maintain a professional appearance.
- **Clarity:** Avoid excessive elements that can clutter the chart. Only include necessary labels, gridlines, and legends.

- **Highlighting Key Data:** Use bold colors or larger fonts to emphasize critical data points or trends.
- **Audience Consideration:** Tailor the level of detail and complexity to the audience's familiarity with the data. For a general audience, simpler charts with clear labels work best.

Real-World Example: Customizing a Sales Performance Chart

Imagine you have a basic column chart displaying monthly sales data. Here's how you can customize it to make it more informative and visually appealing:

1. **Add a Chart Title:** "Monthly Sales Performance 2024."
2. **Customize Axis Titles:** Label the X-axis as "Month" and the Y-axis as "Sales (USD)."
3. **Adjust the Legend:** Position it at the bottom to keep the chart uncluttered.
4. **Add Data Labels:** Place them at the top of each column to show exact sales figures.
5. **Modify Gridlines:** Keep only the primary major horizontal gridlines for clarity.
6. **Format Chart and Plot Areas:** Use a light color for the chart area background and no fill for the plot area to make the columns stand out.

Customizing chart elements in Excel is a powerful way to enhance the communication of your data. By thoughtfully adjusting titles, labels, legends, and formatting, you can create charts that are not only visually appealing but also highly informative. This step-by-step approach ensures your charts effectively convey the insights you want to share, making your data more accessible and engaging for your audience. Whether you're presenting to colleagues, clients, or stakeholders, well-customized charts can significantly elevate the impact of your data visualizations.

6.3 ADVANCED CHART TYPES (PIE, BAR, LINE)

Exploring advanced chart types in Excel opens up a new realm of possibilities for data visualization. Pie, bar, and line charts are among the most versatile and powerful tools for presenting data clearly and effectively. Understanding when and how to use each type can transform your data analysis and presentation skills. Let's dive into each of these advanced chart types, step-by-step.

Pie Charts: Illustrating Proportions

Pie charts are ideal for showing the proportions of a whole. They are visually appealing and can make it easy to see which categories contribute most to the total. Here's how to create and customize a pie chart in Excel.

Step-by-Step Instructions for Pie Charts

1. **Prepare Your Data:** Ensure your data is formatted with categories and their corresponding values. For example:

Category	Value
Marketing	3000
Sales	5000
Development	2000
Support	1000

2. **Select Your Data:** Highlight the data range, in this case, A1.

3. **Insert the Pie Chart:**
   - o Go to the Insert tab on the Excel ribbon.
   - o Click on the Pie Chart icon and choose the type of pie chart you want (e.g., 2-D Pie).

4. **Customize the Pie Chart:**
   - o **Chart Title:** Click on the chart title to edit it and give it a descriptive name, like "Departmental Budget Allocation."
   - o **Data Labels:** To add data labels, go to Chart Tools, click Add Chart Element > Data Labels, and choose a position such as Outside End.
   - o **Legend:** Adjust the legend position if necessary by selecting Add Chart Element > Legend and choosing a new position.

Practical Tips for Pie Charts
   - • **Use Sparingly:** Pie charts are most effective with a small number of categories. Too many slices can make the chart hard to read.
   - • **Highlight Key Slices:** Use contrasting colors or pull out slices to emphasize important categories.

Bar Charts: Comparing Categories

Bar charts are excellent for comparing different categories or groups. They can be used for both vertical and horizontal comparisons. Here's how to create and customize a bar chart in Excel.

Step-by-Step Instructions for Bar Charts

1. **Prepare Your Data:** Your data should have categories and values that you want to compare. For example:

Product	Sales
Product A	1500
Product B	3000
Product C	2000
Product D	2500

2. **Select Your Data:** Highlight the range of cells, A1.

3. **Insert the Bar Chart:**
   - o Navigate to the Insert tab on the Excel ribbon.
   - o Click on the Bar Chart icon and choose a type, such as Clustered Bar.

4. **Customize the Bar Chart:**
   - o **Chart Title:** Click the title to edit and rename it, like "Product Sales Comparison."
   - o **Axis Titles:** Go to Chart Tools, click Add Chart Element > Axis Titles, and add titles for both the horizontal and vertical axes.
   - o **Data Labels:** Add data labels by selecting Add Chart Element > Data Labels and choosing a position like Inside End.

Practical Tips for Bar Charts

- **Consistent Colors:** Use consistent colors to make it easy to compare categories across different charts.
- **Order by Value:** Sorting categories by value can help in quickly identifying the highest and lowest performers.

Line Charts: Showing Trends Over Time

Line charts are perfect for displaying data trends over time. They help in visualizing the progression or changes in data points. Here's how to create and customize a line chart in Excel.

Step-by-Step Instructions for Line Charts

1. **Prepare Your Data:** Ensure your data includes a time series or sequential data points. For example:

Month	Revenue
January	4000
February	4500
March	4200
April	4800
May	5000

2. **Select Your Data:** Highlight the range, A1.

3. **Insert the Line Chart:**
   - Go to the Insert tab on the Excel ribbon.
   - Click on the Line Chart icon and select the type of line chart you want, such as Line with Markers.

4. **Customize the Line Chart:**
   - **Chart Title:** Click on the chart title and rename it, like "Monthly Revenue Trend."
   - **Axis Titles:** Add axis titles by selecting Add Chart Element > Axis Titles for both horizontal and vertical axes.
   - **Data Labels:** Add data labels to display exact values by going to Add Chart Element > Data Labels and choosing Above.

Practical Tips for Line Charts

- **Highlight Key Trends:** Use different line styles or colors to highlight significant trends or changes in the data.
- **Include Markers:** Adding markers can help in identifying specific data points more clearly.

Real-World Examples

Imagine you're a sales manager preparing a report on the performance of different products, departments, and overall revenue trends. Using advanced chart types, you can create a comprehensive visual story:

- **Pie Chart Example:** Illustrate the budget allocation across different departments. By customizing the chart to pull out significant slices, you can emphasize where the majority of resources are allocated.
- **Bar Chart Example:** Compare sales figures of various products. Sorting the bars by sales volume and using consistent colors can quickly highlight top-performing products.
- **Line Chart Example:** Show revenue trends over the first half of the year. Using markers and a clear trend line helps in visualizing the growth trajectory and identifying any anomalies.

Mastering advanced chart types in Excel enables you to present data in a more compelling and insightful manner. By understanding the unique strengths of pie, bar, and line charts, you can choose the most appropriate type for your data and customize it to communicate your message effectively. Whether you are presenting to a team, reporting to management, or analyzing trends for decision-making, these advanced charts are invaluable tools in your Excel toolkit. Practice creating and customizing these charts to enhance your data visualization skills and make your presentations stand out.

7. WORKING WITH PIVOTTABLES

Imagine you're sitting at your desk, staring at a massive spreadsheet filled with rows and rows of data. It's overwhelming, right? Now, imagine if there was a way to quickly summarize, analyze, and make sense of all that information with just a few clicks. Enter PivotTables—Excel's powerful tool for transforming unwieldy data into meaningful insights.

PivotTables are like magic wands for data analysis. They allow you to pivot, or rearrange, your data dynamically to see it from different perspectives. Whether you need to summarize sales figures by region, analyze expense reports by category, or compare product performance over time, PivotTables can do it all. They enable you to slice and dice your data, making it easier to uncover patterns, spot trends, and make data-driven decisions.

Creating a PivotTable might seem intimidating at first, but it's surprisingly straightforward once you get the hang of it. Think of it as setting up a new perspective on your data. You start by selecting the range of data you want to analyze. Then, with a few simple steps, you can drag and drop fields to arrange them into a table that highlights the information you need.

One of the most powerful aspects of PivotTables is their flexibility. You can quickly adjust your view by moving fields around, applying filters, and adding calculated fields. This means you can answer different questions about your data without creating multiple static reports. It's all about making your data work for you, rather than the other way around.

In this chapter, we'll explore the world of PivotTables, from basic setup to advanced customization. You'll learn how to create PivotTables, customize them to your needs, and use them to extract valuable insights from your data. By the end, you'll be equipped with the skills to turn complex data into clear, actionable information—an invaluable asset in any data-driven environment. So, let's dive in and discover the power of PivotTables!

7.1 INTRODUCTION TO PIVOTTABLES

Imagine you have a sprawling spreadsheet filled with sales data from various regions, product categories, and time periods. It's a goldmine of information, but finding the nuggets of insight buried within can be daunting. This is where PivotTables come to your rescue. PivotTables are Excel's powerhouse feature, designed to help you summarize, analyze, and explore your data efficiently. They transform rows and columns of data into a meaningful report in just a few clicks.

What is a PivotTable?

A PivotTable is an interactive table that allows you to group and summarize large amounts of data quickly and easily. It enables you to rearrange, or "pivot," data to view it from different perspectives. Whether you want to see total sales by region, average sales per product, or compare quarterly sales figures, a PivotTable can handle it all. Think of it as a dynamic report that can adapt to your analysis needs.

Setting Up Your First PivotTable

Creating a PivotTable starts with selecting your data. Here's a step-by-step guide to get you started:

1. **Prepare Your Data:** Ensure your data is organized in a tabular format with headers for each column. For example, a sales report might include columns for Date, Region, Product, and Sales Amount.

2. **Select Your Data Range:** Click anywhere within your data range. If your data is structured as an Excel Table, you can simply click inside the table.

3. **Insert a PivotTable:** Go to the Insert tab on the ribbon and click on PivotTable. Excel will prompt you to confirm the data range and ask where you want the PivotTable to be placed—either in a new worksheet or an existing one.

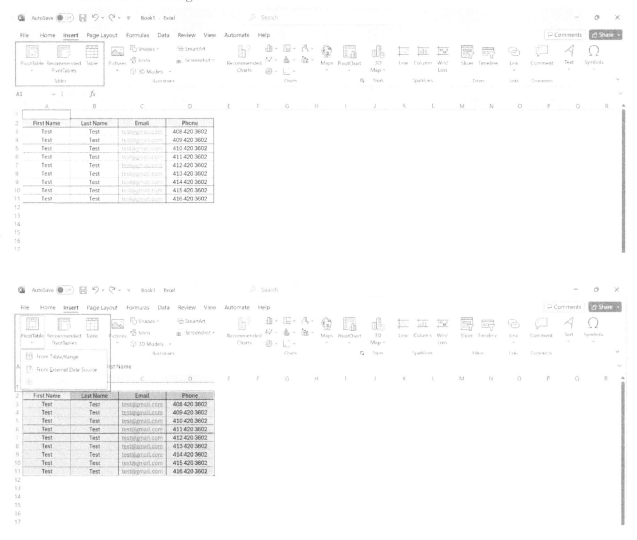

Building Your PivotTable

Once the PivotTable is created, a new pane called the PivotTable Fields List will appear on the right side of your Excel window. This is where the magic happens. The fields from your data set are listed here, ready for you to drag and drop into the different areas of the PivotTable.

- **Rows:** Drag fields here to create row labels. For instance, dragging the Region field to the Rows area will list each region in your data.

- **Columns:** Drag fields here to create column labels. Adding the Quarter field to Columns might break down your data by each quarter.

- **Values:** This is where the calculations occur. Drag numeric fields, like Sales Amount, here to see totals, averages, or other calculations.

- **Filters:** Use this area to add fields that you want to filter by. For example, dragging Product Category here allows you to filter the entire PivotTable by different product categories.

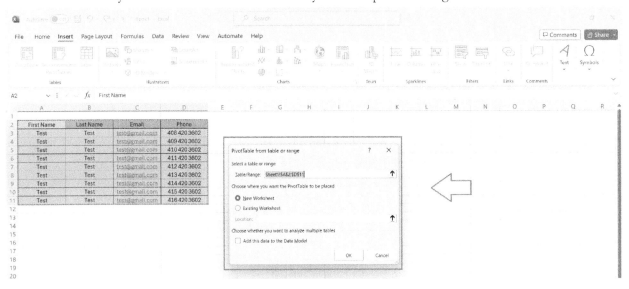

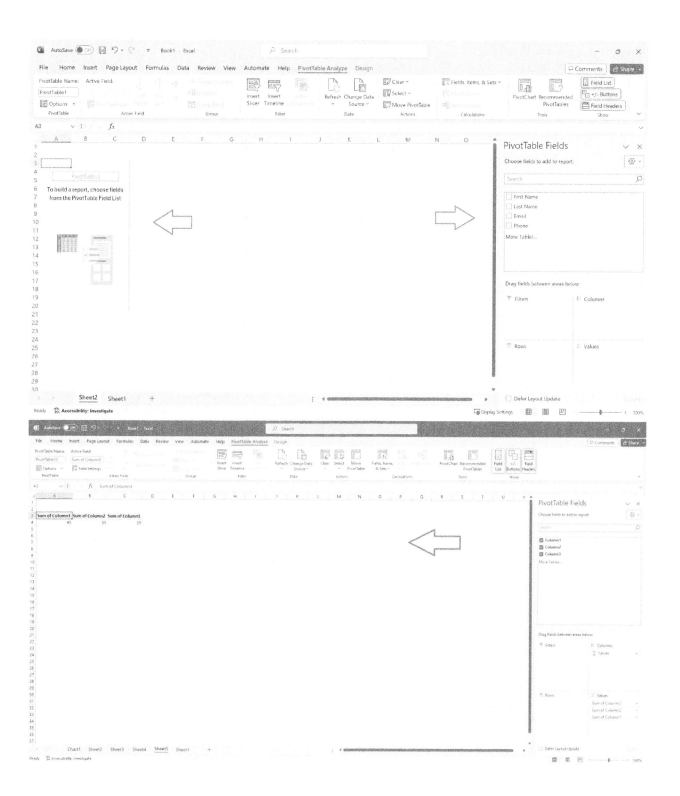

Customizing Your PivotTable

Customization is key to making your PivotTable as useful as possible. Here are some essential customization techniques:

- **Sorting and Filtering:** Click the dropdown arrows on the Row or Column labels to sort your data or apply filters. This helps you focus on the most relevant information.
- **Value Field Settings:** Click on any value in the Values area and select Value Field Settings to change the summary function. For example, you can switch from Sum to Average, Count, Max, or Min.
- **Grouping Data:** Right-click on any field in the PivotTable and select Group to group data. You can group dates by months, quarters, or years, and numeric data into ranges.

Practical Tips for Using PivotTables

- **Start Simple:** When creating your first PivotTable, start with basic fields and gradually add complexity. This helps you understand how the data interacts.
- **Use Slicers:** Slicers are visual filters that make it easy to filter data in your PivotTable. They are particularly useful when you want to create interactive reports. To add a slicer, go to the Insert tab, click Slicer, and choose the field you want to use as a filter.
- **Refresh Your Data:** If your source data changes, you can refresh the PivotTable to reflect these updates. Right-click on the PivotTable and select Refresh.

Real-World Example: Analyzing Sales Data

Let's consider a practical example. Suppose you have a dataset of sales transactions with columns for Date, Region, Product, and Sales Amount. You want to analyze which region has the highest sales and which products are the top sellers.

1. **Insert a PivotTable:** Select your data range and insert a PivotTable in a new worksheet.
2. **Set Rows and Values:** Drag the Region field to the Rows area and the Sales Amount field to the Values area. Instantly, you'll see the total sales for each region.
3. **Add Columns for Deeper Insight:** Drag the Product field to the Columns area. Now, your PivotTable shows sales totals for each product in each region.
4. **Filter by Date:** Add the Date field to the Filters area. This allows you to filter the entire table by specific dates or date ranges.

Advanced Customization: Calculated Fields and Items

For more complex analysis, you can use calculated fields and items within your PivotTable. Calculated fields allow you to create new data fields based on existing ones, while calculated items enable you to perform calculations within the data items.

- **Adding a Calculated Field:** Go to the PivotTable Analyze tab, click Fields, Items & Sets, and select Calculated Field. You can create a new field, such as Profit, by subtracting Cost from Sales.

- **Using Calculated Items:** Right-click on a field in your PivotTable, select Show Field List, then under the field, click on Field Settings, and choose Add Calculated Item. This is useful for performing calculations like year-over-year growth.

PivotTables are indispensable tools for anyone dealing with large datasets. They provide a flexible and powerful way to analyze and present data, making it easier to draw insights and make informed decisions. By mastering the basics of creating and customizing PivotTables, you can turn complex data into clear, actionable reports. Whether you are a beginner or looking to refine your skills, understanding PivotTables will significantly enhance your data analysis capabilities in Excel. So, dive in, experiment with different configurations, and see how PivotTables can transform your data into meaningful insights.

7.2 CREATING AND CUSTOMIZING PIVOTTABLES

Imagine you're about to uncover the hidden stories within your data. Creating and customizing PivotTables in Excel is like being a detective, piecing together clues to reveal valuable insights. Let's delve into the process of building and refining PivotTables to make your data analysis not just easier, but truly powerful.

Step-by-Step Guide to Creating a PivotTable

Selecting and Preparing Your Data

Your journey with PivotTables begins with selecting the right data. Make sure your data is in a structured format, with each column having a clear header. This ensures that Excel recognizes the different fields when you create your PivotTable.

1. **Choose Your Data Range:** Click anywhere within your dataset. If your data is in an Excel Table, you're ready to go. If not, simply select the range of data you want to analyze.
2. **Insert the PivotTable:** Navigate to the Insert tab on the Excel ribbon and click PivotTable. A dialog box will appear, asking you to confirm the data range and choose where to place the PivotTable. You can opt to place it in a new worksheet or an existing one.

Building the PivotTable

With your data ready and the PivotTable inserted, the real fun begins. The PivotTable Fields pane will appear, allowing you to drag and drop fields into four main areas: Filters, Columns, Rows, and Values.

1. **Drag Fields to Rows and Columns:** Start by dragging the fields you want to analyze into the Rows and Columns areas. For example, if you're analyzing sales data, you might drag Region to Rows and Quarter to Columns.
2. **Add Data to Values:** Next, drag a numeric field, such as Sales Amount, to the Values area. By default, Excel will sum these values, but you can change the summary function to average, count, or other calculations.
3. **Apply Filters if Needed:** If you want to focus on specific subsets of your data, drag fields to the Filters area. This could be useful for isolating data by product category or time period.

Customizing Your PivotTable

Customization transforms a basic PivotTable into a tailored, insightful report. Here's how you can refine your PivotTable to better meet your analysis needs.

Adjusting Field Settings

The settings for each field in your PivotTable can be adjusted to better summarize your data.

1. **Change Value Field Settings:** Click on the drop-down arrow next to a value field in the Values area, then select Value Field Settings. Here, you can choose different functions like Sum, Average, Count, Max, or Min.
2. **Rename Fields:** Make your PivotTable easier to understand by renaming fields. Simply click the field name in the PivotTable and type a new, more descriptive name.

Sorting and Filtering Data

Sorting and filtering help to highlight the most important data in your PivotTable.

1. **Sort Data:** Click the drop-down arrow next to a Row or Column label and select Sort A to Z or Sort Z to A. This arranges your data in ascending or descending order.
2. **Filter Data:** Use the drop-down menus in the Filters area to include or exclude specific data points. For example, you might filter out a particular region to focus on others.

Grouping Data

Grouping can simplify your analysis by consolidating similar data points. This is especially useful for dates and numeric ranges.

1. **Group by Date:** Right-click on any date field in the PivotTable and choose Group. You can group by days, months, quarters, or years to summarize your data over different time periods.
2. **Group Numeric Data:** Similarly, right-click on numeric fields and select Group. You can define ranges to categorize your data, such as grouping sales amounts into intervals.

Practical Tips for Effective Customization

- **Use Slicers for Interactive Filtering:** Slicers are visual tools that make filtering data interactive and intuitive. To add a slicer, go to the Insert tab, click Slicer, and select the field you want to filter by. This adds clickable buttons to filter your PivotTable dynamically.
- **Conditional Formatting:** Highlight key data points using conditional formatting. Select the data you want to format, go to the Home tab, and choose Conditional Formatting. Apply rules to change cell colors based on value thresholds, making important data stand out.
- **Refresh Your PivotTable:** If your source data changes, you can refresh the PivotTable to update it with the latest data. Right-click on the PivotTable and select Refresh.

Real-World Example: Customizing a Sales Analysis PivotTable

Imagine you have a dataset of sales transactions, and you want to analyze sales performance by region and product category over the past year.

1. **Insert the PivotTable:** Select your dataset and insert a PivotTable in a new worksheet.
2. **Set Rows and Columns:** Drag Region to the Rows area and Product Category to the Columns area.
3. **Add Sales Data:** Drag Sales Amount to the Values area to see total sales.
4. **Apply Filters:** Add Date to the Filters area and filter to show only data from the past year.
5. **Group Dates:** Right-click on the Date field in the Rows area and group by quarters to see quarterly sales performance.
6. **Use Slicers:** Add slicers for Region and Product Category to make it easy to filter the PivotTable interactively.
7. **Apply Conditional Formatting:** Highlight top-performing regions and products using conditional formatting to quickly identify key insights.

Creating and customizing PivotTables in Excel is a powerful way to turn raw data into meaningful, actionable insights. By following these steps and leveraging customization options, you can build dynamic reports that help you make data-driven decisions with confidence. Practice these techniques to become proficient in using PivotTables, and you'll find that analyzing complex datasets becomes not only manageable but also enjoyable. Whether you're preparing reports for stakeholders or exploring data trends, PivotTables will be your go-to tool for efficient and effective data analysis.

7.3 ANALYZING DATA WITH PIVOTTABLES

Analyzing data with PivotTables in Excel is like having a Swiss Army knife for data interpretation. These versatile tools allow you to extract meaningful insights from your data, enabling you to make informed decisions swiftly and accurately. Let's explore how to analyze data effectively using PivotTables, breaking down the process into clear, actionable steps.

Understanding the Basics of Data Analysis with PivotTables

PivotTables provide a dynamic way to summarize and explore your data. Unlike static tables, PivotTables let you pivot—or rearrange—the data to view it from different perspectives. This flexibility is crucial for uncovering trends, identifying patterns, and making comparisons.

Setting Up Your Data for Analysis

Before diving into analysis, ensure your data is well-prepared. Clean, structured data leads to more accurate and meaningful PivotTable results.

1. **Organize Your Data:** Your data should be in a tabular format, with clear headers for each column. Avoid blank rows or columns within your dataset.
2. **Select Your Data Range:** Click within your data range to prepare for creating a PivotTable.

Creating the PivotTable

Start by creating a PivotTable, which serves as your canvas for analysis.

1. **Insert the PivotTable:** Navigate to the Insert tab on the ribbon and select PivotTable. Excel will prompt you to choose your data range and the location for the PivotTable. Opt for a new worksheet for a cleaner workspace.
2. **Configure the PivotTable:** Drag and drop fields into the Rows, Columns, Values, and Filters areas to start shaping your data.

Analyzing Data with PivotTables

Summarizing Data

Summarizing data is the foundation of analysis. PivotTables can quickly aggregate data to show totals, averages, counts, and more.

1. **Drag Fields to Values:** To summarize data, drag a numeric field, such as Sales Amount, into the Values area. By default, Excel will sum these values, but you can change this by selecting Value Field Settings and choosing a different function, such as average or count.
2. **Customize the Summary:** Rename fields to make your PivotTable more understandable. Click on the field name in the PivotTable and type a new name.

Filtering Data

Filtering helps you focus on specific subsets of your data, making it easier to analyze particular aspects.

1. **Use Filters:** Drag relevant fields into the Filters area. For instance, if analyzing sales, you might add Product Category to filter by specific products.

2. **Apply Slicers:** Slicers provide a visual and interactive way to filter data. To add a slicer, go to the Insert tab, click Slicer, and select the field you want to filter by.

Grouping Data

Grouping data allows you to consolidate similar items for better analysis. This is particularly useful for date and numeric fields.

1. **Group Dates:** Right-click on a date field in the PivotTable and select Group. You can group by days, months, quarters, or years to summarize time-based data effectively.

2. **Group Numeric Data:** Right-click on a numeric field and select Group. Define ranges to categorize your data into meaningful intervals.

Exploring Trends and Patterns

PivotTables excel at revealing trends and patterns in your data.

1. **Analyze Time-Based Trends:** By grouping data by time periods (e.g., months or quarters), you can observe trends over time. Drag the date field to Rows, and sales data to Values, then group by months to see monthly sales trends.

2. **Identify Patterns:** Look for recurring patterns by comparing different segments. For instance, compare sales performance across regions by dragging Region to Rows and Sales Amount to Values.

Using Calculated Fields and Items

For more advanced analysis, calculated fields and items enable you to create new data based on existing fields.

1. **Add a Calculated Field:** Go to the PivotTable Analyze tab, click Fields, Items & Sets, then select Calculated Field. Create new metrics, such as profit, by defining a formula that subtracts costs from sales.

2. **Create Calculated Items:** Right-click on a field and select Show Field List. Under the field, click Field Settings and choose Add Calculated Item. This allows you to perform custom calculations within a field.

Real-World Example: Sales Performance Analysis

Imagine you're analyzing sales performance for different products across various regions. Here's how you can use a PivotTable to gain insights:

1. **Insert the PivotTable:** Select your sales dataset and insert a PivotTable in a new worksheet.

2. **Set Up Rows and Columns:** Drag Region to Rows and Product to Columns.

3. **Summarize Sales Data:** Drag Sales Amount to Values. You now see total sales for each product in each region.

4. **Filter by Date:** Add the Date field to Filters and filter by the current year to focus on recent sales performance.

5. **Group by Quarter:** Group the Date field by quarters to analyze quarterly performance.
6. **Add a Slicer:** Insert a slicer for Region to easily filter data by different regions.

Practical Tips for Effective Data Analysis

- **Keep It Simple:** Start with basic summaries and gradually add complexity. This helps you build a clear understanding before diving into advanced analysis.
- **Use Visual Cues:** Conditional formatting can highlight key data points. Apply color scales or data bars to make important values stand out.
- **Refresh Regularly:** If your source data updates, refresh the PivotTable to ensure your analysis reflects the latest information.

Analyzing data with PivotTables in Excel unlocks a powerful capability to interpret and understand your data. By summarizing, filtering, grouping, and using calculated fields, you can transform raw data into actionable insights. This process not only enhances your data analysis skills but also enables you to make data-driven decisions confidently. Practice these techniques to become proficient in using PivotTables, and you'll find yourself equipped to tackle any data analysis challenge with ease. Whether you're preparing reports, exploring business trends, or making strategic decisions, PivotTables will be your indispensable tool for effective data analysis.

8. Excel Tips and Shortcuts

Imagine Excel as a vast toolbox, each feature a unique tool waiting to be discovered. While mastering the fundamental tools is crucial, knowing the hidden tips and shortcuts can transform you from a proficient user into an Excel wizard. In this chapter, we will delve into these lesser-known yet incredibly powerful techniques that can save you time, reduce errors, and make your work more efficient and enjoyable.

Excel is packed with shortcuts and tricks that can streamline your workflow. Picture yourself effortlessly navigating through spreadsheets, manipulating data with ease, and creating complex formulas in seconds. These shortcuts are not just about speeding up your tasks; they are about enhancing your overall Excel experience, allowing you to focus on the insights rather than the mechanics.

Consider the last time you spent hours manually formatting cells or entering repetitive data. What if you could automate those processes, leaving you with more time to analyze and interpret your data? That's the magic of Excel shortcuts and tips. From keyboard shortcuts that make navigation a breeze to clever tricks that simplify data entry and formatting, these tools are designed to make your life easier.

In this chapter, you'll discover practical tips that can help you avoid common pitfalls and mistakes. You'll learn how to customize Excel to fit your specific needs, making it a truly personalized tool. Whether you're a beginner eager to improve your skills or an experienced user looking to refine your techniques, these tips and shortcuts will elevate your Excel game.

Join me as we unlock the secrets of Excel's efficiency. By the end of this chapter, you'll not only work faster but also smarter, mastering Excel in ways you never thought possible. So, let's dive in and explore the treasure trove of Excel tips and shortcuts that will transform your spreadsheet experience.

8.1 Keyboard Shortcuts for Efficiency

Imagine sitting at your desk, fingers flying over the keyboard, performing complex Excel tasks in mere seconds. This isn't a scene from a movie—it's the power of mastering keyboard shortcuts. Using shortcuts not only saves time but also keeps your workflow seamless, reducing the need to switch between the keyboard and mouse constantly. Let's dive into some essential keyboard shortcuts that will significantly boost your efficiency in Excel 2024.

Navigating the Spreadsheet

Navigating large spreadsheets can be a daunting task, but with the right shortcuts, you can move around with ease.

1. **Moving Between Cells:**
   - **Arrow Keys:** Use the arrow keys to move one cell at a time in any direction.
   - **Ctrl + Arrow Keys:** Jump to the edge of the data region in any direction. This is particularly useful for quickly reaching the end of a dataset.
2. **Scrolling Through Worksheets:**
   - **Ctrl + Page Up/Page Down:** Quickly switch between different worksheets within your workbook. This saves time when working with multiple sheets.

Selecting Data

Efficient data selection is critical for many Excel tasks, from formatting to formula application.

1. **Selecting a Range of Cells:**
    o   **Shift + Arrow Keys:** Extend your selection one cell at a time.
    o   **Ctrl + Shift + Arrow Keys:** Extend your selection to the edge of the data region.
2. **Selecting Entire Rows and Columns:**
    o   **Shift + Space:** Select the entire row of the active cell.
    o   **Ctrl + Space:** Select the entire column of the active cell.

Editing and Formatting

Quick editing and formatting can significantly enhance your productivity.

1. **Copying and Pasting:**
    o   **Ctrl + C:** Copy selected cells.
    o   **Ctrl + V:** Paste copied cells.
    o   **Ctrl + X:** Cut selected cells.
    o   **Ctrl + Alt + V:** Open the Paste Special dialog box to choose specific paste options.
2. **Undo and Redo:**
    o   **Ctrl + Z:** Undo the last action.
    o   **Ctrl + Y:** Redo the last undone action.
3. **Formatting Cells:**
    o   **Ctrl + 1:** Open the Format Cells dialog box.
    o   **Ctrl + B:** Bold the selected text.
    o   **Ctrl + I:** Italicize the selected text.
    o   **Ctrl + U:** Underline the selected text.

Working with Formulas

Formulas are the backbone of Excel, and knowing shortcuts for working with them can greatly enhance your efficiency.

1. **Entering Formulas:**
    o   **Equals (=):** Start a formula.
    o   **Alt + Equals (Alt + =):** Quickly sum a column or row of numbers with the AutoSum function.
2. **Editing Formulas:**
    o   **F2:** Edit the active cell's contents, placing the cursor at the end of the text.
    o   **Ctrl + ` (Ctrl + Grave Accent):** Toggle between displaying cell values and formulas.

Managing Workbooks

Managing multiple workbooks is a common task that can be streamlined with the right shortcuts.

1. **Opening and Saving Workbooks:**
   - **Ctrl + N:** Create a new workbook.
   - **Ctrl + O:** Open an existing workbook.
   - **Ctrl + S:** Save the current workbook.
   - **F12:** Open the Save As dialog box.

2. **Closing Workbooks:**
   - **Ctrl + W:** Close the current workbook.
   - **Ctrl + Q:** Quit Excel.

Practical Tips for Mastering Keyboard Shortcuts

1. **Practice Regularly:** The more you use these shortcuts, the more instinctive they become. Start by incorporating a few at a time into your daily routine.
2. **Create a Cheat Sheet:** Keep a list of frequently used shortcuts nearby until you've memorized them.
3. **Use the Ribbon Key Tips:** Press the Alt key to display shortcut keys for ribbon commands, helping you navigate through options without a mouse.

Real-World Example: Streamlining Data Entry

Let's consider a scenario where you need to enter and format a large set of data efficiently.

1. **Enter Data Quickly:** Use the arrow keys and Tab to move between cells as you enter data.
2. **Select and Format Cells:**
   - After entering data, use **Ctrl + Shift + Arrow Keys** to select the entire dataset.
   - Press **Ctrl + 1** to open the Format Cells dialog box and apply necessary formatting, such as setting number formats or adding borders.
3. **Copy and Paste Data:**
   - Copy data from one section using **Ctrl + C** and paste it to another location with **Ctrl + V**.
   - Use **Ctrl + Alt + V** for Paste Special options to ensure data is pasted in the desired format.

Mastering keyboard shortcuts in Excel transforms your workflow, making you faster and more efficient. These shortcuts reduce the time spent on repetitive tasks, allowing you to focus on analyzing data and deriving insights. By incorporating these shortcuts into your daily Excel use, you'll not only enhance your productivity but also gain a deeper understanding of Excel's powerful capabilities. Practice regularly, create a cheat sheet, and soon you'll find yourself navigating and manipulating data with the finesse of an Excel expert. Let's embrace these shortcuts and unlock the full potential of Excel 2024!

8.2 TIME-SAVING TIPS AND TRICKS

Imagine having the power to breeze through complex Excel tasks, freeing up valuable time for deeper analysis and strategic thinking. In this section, we'll uncover a collection of time-saving tips and tricks that can transform how you work with Excel 2024. These techniques are designed to streamline your workflow, reduce repetitive tasks, and make your overall Excel experience more efficient.

Flash Fill: Automating Data Entry

Flash Fill is like having a smart assistant that learns your patterns and fills in the rest. It's perfect for formatting data quickly without using complex formulas.

1. **Activate Flash Fill:** Start typing the desired format in the adjacent column. For example, if you have a list of names in the format "John Doe" and you want to separate them into two columns, start typing "John" in the first cell.
2. **Invoke Flash Fill:** As you type the second example, Excel will recognize the pattern and suggest the remaining entries. Press Enter to accept the suggestions or use Ctrl + E to activate Flash Fill manually.

AutoSum: Quick Calculations

The AutoSum feature is a quick way to perform basic calculations such as sum, average, and count without manually entering formulas.

1. **Select the Cell:** Click the cell where you want the result to appear.
2. **Use AutoSum:** Go to the Home tab and click on the AutoSum button. Excel will automatically select the range of cells to be summed. Press Enter to complete the calculation.

Quick Analysis Tool: Instant Data Visualization

The Quick Analysis tool provides instant access to formatting, charts, totals, tables, and sparklines based on your selected data.

1. **Highlight Your Data:** Select the range of data you want to analyze.
2. **Activate Quick Analysis:** Click the Quick Analysis button that appears at the bottom right of your selection or press Ctrl + Q.
3. **Choose an Option:** Explore various options such as Formatting, Charts, Totals, Tables, and Sparklines to quickly visualize and analyze your data.

Conditional Formatting: Highlighting Important Data

Conditional Formatting automatically changes the appearance of cells based on specified conditions, making it easier to spot trends and outliers.

1. **Select Your Data Range:** Highlight the cells you want to format.
2. **Apply Conditional Formatting:** Go to the Home tab, click on Conditional Formatting, and choose a rule type. For example, to highlight cells greater than a certain value, select Highlight Cell Rules > Greater Than, and set your criteria.

Remove Duplicates: Cleaning Up Data

Removing duplicates is essential for ensuring data accuracy and reliability.

1. **Select the Data Range:** Highlight the range that you want to clean up.
2. **Remove Duplicates:** Go to the Data tab and click on Remove Duplicates. Choose the columns to check for duplicates and click OK. Excel will remove duplicate entries, leaving a clean dataset.

Data Validation: Ensuring Data Accuracy

Data validation helps maintain data integrity by restricting the type of data that can be entered into a cell.

1. **Select the Cells for Validation:** Highlight the cells you want to restrict.
2. **Apply Data Validation:** Go to the Data tab, click on Data Validation, and set your criteria. For example, to restrict entries to whole numbers between 1 and 100, choose Whole Number from the Allow dropdown, and set the Minimum and Maximum values.

Named Ranges: Simplifying Formulas

Named ranges make your formulas easier to understand and manage by allowing you to refer to cells or ranges with meaningful names.

1. **Define a Named Range:** Select the cells you want to name, go to the Formulas tab, and click on Define Name. Enter a meaningful name, such as "SalesData", and click OK.
2. **Use Named Ranges in Formulas:** Instead of referencing cells directly in formulas, use the named range. For example, =SUM(SalesData) is much clearer than =SUM(A1:A10).

Real-World Example: Streamlining a Monthly Report

Imagine you need to prepare a monthly sales report. These time-saving tricks can significantly speed up the process:

1. **Use Flash Fill:** Quickly format dates or names. If you have dates in the format "20240101" (YYYYMMDD) and want to change them to "01/01/2024", type the first date in the new format and use Flash Fill to complete the column.
2. **AutoSum for Totals:** Use AutoSum to quickly calculate total sales for each month.
3. **Quick Analysis Tool for Visualization:** Highlight your sales data and use the Quick Analysis tool to add charts or data bars that visually represent sales trends.
4. **Conditional Formatting to Highlight Key Figures:** Apply conditional formatting to highlight sales figures that exceed targets.
5. **Remove Duplicates for Clean Data:** Ensure your sales data is accurate by removing any duplicate entries.
6. **Data Validation for Accurate Entries:** Set up data validation to ensure that all sales entries fall within the expected range.
7. **Named Ranges for Clarity:** Define named ranges for different datasets within your report, making your formulas easier to read and manage.

Mastering these time-saving tips and tricks in Excel 2024 will transform how you work with data. By automating repetitive tasks and leveraging powerful tools like Flash Fill, AutoSum, and the Quick Analysis tool, you'll not only save time but also enhance the accuracy and clarity of your reports. Conditional formatting and data validation help maintain data integrity, while named ranges simplify complex formulas. Incorporate these techniques into your daily workflow to unlock a more efficient and enjoyable Excel experience. Whether you're preparing detailed reports or performing quick data checks, these tips and tricks will help you achieve more with less effort, making you a true Excel pro.

8.3 COMMON MISTAKES AND HOW TO AVOID THEM

Using Excel effectively requires not only mastering its features but also being aware of common pitfalls. Even experienced users can fall into traps that lead to errors, inefficiencies, and frustration. By identifying these common mistakes and learning how to avoid them, you can enhance your productivity and ensure the accuracy of your work. Let's delve into some typical errors and provide practical solutions to keep your Excel experience smooth and efficient.

Misusing Cell References

One of the most frequent mistakes in Excel is misusing cell references, which can lead to incorrect calculations and errors.

Absolute vs. Relative References

1. **Understanding the Difference:**
   - **Relative References:** Change when a formula is copied to another cell (e.g., A1).
   - **Absolute References:** Remain constant, regardless of where the formula is copied (e.g., A1).
2. **Avoiding the Mistake:**
   - **Identify Your Needs:** Determine if you need the reference to change or stay constant. For instance, when calculating percentages across a range, an absolute reference to the total cell ensures consistency.

Step-by-Step Guide

1. **Use F4 to Toggle References:**
   - When entering a formula, press F4 after selecting a cell reference to toggle between relative and absolute references.
2. **Practical Tip:**
   - For mixed references (e.g., A$1 or $A1), use F4 to cycle through the options until the desired reference type is set.

Incorrect Formula Ranges

Selecting incorrect ranges for your formulas can produce misleading results.

Using Named Ranges
1. **Define Named Ranges:**
   o Select the range you want to name, go to the Formulas tab, and click on Define Name. Enter a meaningful name (e.g., SalesData).
2. **Incorporate Named Ranges in Formulas:**
   o Instead of manually selecting a range, use the named range in your formulas (e.g., =SUM(SalesData)).

Step-by-Step Guide
1. **Check Your Ranges:**
   o Double-check the ranges selected in your formulas. Click on the formula cell and ensure the highlighted range covers all necessary data.
2. **Practical Tip:**
   o Use the Name Manager in the Formulas tab to review and manage all named ranges in your workbook.

Ignoring Data Validation

Skipping data validation can lead to inconsistent and inaccurate data entry.

Setting Up Data Validation
1. **Implement Data Validation:**
   o Select the cells you want to validate, go to the Data tab, and click on Data Validation. Set criteria for the data (e.g., whole numbers between 1 and 100).
2. **Customize Error Messages:**
   o Provide clear error messages to guide users on the correct data entry.

Step-by-Step Guide
1. **Apply Validation Rules:**
   o Choose the validation criteria that fit your data requirements. For instance, to restrict entries to dates within a certain range, select Date and specify the range.
2. **Practical Tip:**
   o Use the Input Message tab in the Data Validation dialog to provide users with instructions before they enter data.

Overcomplicating Formulas

Complex formulas can be difficult to understand, troubleshoot, and maintain.

Simplifying Formulas

1. **Break Down Complex Formulas:**
   o Split complex calculations into simpler, intermediate steps across multiple cells.
2. **Use Functions Effectively:**
   o Utilize built-in functions to simplify calculations (e.g., use SUMIFS instead of nested IF statements).

Step-by-Step Guide

1. **Decompose Formulas:**
   o If a formula becomes too long, break it down into smaller parts. For example, calculate each component separately before combining them.
2. **Practical Tip:**
   o Document complex formulas with comments. Select the cell, press Shift + F2, and add explanations to clarify the purpose of each part of the formula.

Neglecting Regular Data Backups

Failing to back up your data can result in significant losses if your file becomes corrupted or accidentally deleted.

Automating Backups

1. **Enable AutoSave:**
   o Use Excel's AutoSave feature for cloud-based workbooks stored in OneDrive or SharePoint.
2. **Create Manual Backups:**
   o Regularly save copies of your workbook with version numbers (e.g., SalesReport_V1, SalesReport_V2).

Step-by-Step Guide

1. **Set Up AutoSave:**
   o Ensure your workbook is saved in OneDrive or SharePoint and enable AutoSave from the top toolbar.
2. **Practical Tip:**
   o Periodically use File > Save As to create backup versions. This practice helps track changes and recover previous versions if needed.

Real-World Example: Avoiding Common Pitfalls in a Financial Report

Imagine you're preparing a financial report. Here's how you can avoid common mistakes:

1. **Use Absolute References:**
   o When calculating the percentage contribution of each department to the total budget, use absolute references to the total cell to ensure consistency.

2. **Check Formula Ranges:**
   o Double-check that your SUM ranges include all relevant cells, especially if the data is dynamic and regularly updated.

3. **Implement Data Validation:**
   o Ensure only valid expense entries by setting up data validation for each cost category.

4. **Simplify Complex Formulas:**
   o Break down the total expenditure calculation into smaller parts, such as individual department totals, before summing them up.

5. **Backup Regularly:**
   o Enable AutoSave for your report saved in OneDrive and periodically create manual backups to track progress and changes.

Avoiding common mistakes in Excel not only improves the accuracy and reliability of your data but also enhances your efficiency and confidence. By mastering cell references, formula ranges, data validation, simplifying complex formulas, and ensuring regular backups, you can prevent errors that often plague even experienced users. Implement these strategies into your workflow to create robust, error-free spreadsheets that stand up to scrutiny. Excel is a powerful tool, and with these precautions, you can harness its full potential while minimizing the risk of common pitfalls. Embrace these practices to transform your Excel experience and achieve greater success in your data-driven tasks.

9. DATA ANALYSIS TOOLS

Imagine standing at the edge of a vast ocean of data, each wave representing endless possibilities and insights waiting to be discovered. Excel's data analysis tools are your navigational compass, designed to guide you through this ocean, transforming raw data into meaningful patterns and actionable information. In this chapter, we will embark on a journey through some of the most powerful data analysis tools that Excel has to offer, equipping you with the skills to uncover hidden trends, make informed decisions, and predict future outcomes with confidence.

Data analysis in Excel is like detective work—sifting through information, identifying clues, and piecing together a coherent story that drives strategic decisions. Whether you are a business professional analyzing sales trends, a financial analyst evaluating investment opportunities, or a student seeking to understand research data, mastering these tools will elevate your analytical capabilities.

Excel's data analysis tools are not just about crunching numbers; they are about revealing insights that would otherwise remain hidden. Tools like Goal Seek, Solver, and the Analysis ToolPak allow you to perform sophisticated analyses without needing a degree in statistics. They simplify complex calculations and enable you to model various scenarios, optimize outcomes, and validate your assumptions.

Consider the last time you faced a challenging decision with multiple variables. What if you could simulate different scenarios and see the potential outcomes before making a choice? Excel's data analysis tools empower you to do just that, providing clarity and foresight.

In this chapter, you'll learn how to harness these tools effectively, from basic statistical analysis to advanced optimization techniques. By the end, you'll be able to turn data into a strategic asset, driving your projects and decisions with precision and insight. So, let's set sail and explore the powerful world of Excel's data analysis tools, where data-driven decision-making becomes second nature.

9.1 USING DATA ANALYSIS TOOLS (GOAL SEEK, SOLVER)

Picture yourself as an explorer in the vast landscape of data, armed with tools that can predict outcomes and optimize decisions. Excel's Goal Seek and Solver are two such powerful tools that transform your data analysis capabilities, allowing you to forecast, find solutions to complex problems, and make informed decisions with ease. Let's dive into how you can use these tools to unlock the full potential of your data.

Goal Seek: Finding the Desired Result

Goal Seek is like having a crystal ball that tells you the exact input needed to achieve a specific outcome. It's perfect for scenarios where you know the result you want but need to determine the necessary input.

Step-by-Step Guide to Using Goal Seek

1. **Identify Your Target Value:**
   o Suppose you want to find out what sales volume is needed to reach a specific revenue target. Your formula for revenue might be =Sales Volume * Unit Price.

2. **Set Up Your Data:**
   - o Let's say your current sales volume is in cell A1, the unit price in cell A2, and the revenue formula in cell A3 (=A1*A2).
3. **Access Goal Seek:**
   - o Go to the Data tab, click on What-If Analysis, and select Goal Seek.
4. **Define the Parameters:**
   - o In the Goal Seek dialog box, set the following:
     - ▪ **Set cell:** Enter the cell with the formula (A3).
     - ▪ **To value:** Enter your target revenue (e.g., 5000).
     - ▪ **By changing cell:** Enter the cell with the variable you want to adjust (A1).
5. **Execute Goal Seek:**
   - o Click OK, and Excel will adjust the sales volume in cell A1 until the revenue in cell A3 matches your target.

Practical Tips for Goal Seek

- • **Precision Matters:** Ensure your formulas are accurate and your initial data is correctly entered.
- • **Single Variable Focus:** Goal Seek works best when adjusting one variable. For more complex scenarios, consider using Solver.

Solver: Optimizing Complex Problems

Solver is like an advanced version of Goal Seek, allowing you to optimize multiple variables within constraints. It's ideal for more complex decision-making scenarios, such as maximizing profits, minimizing costs, or finding the best combination of inputs.

Step-by-Step Guide to Using Solver

1. **Define the Problem:**
   - o Imagine you need to maximize profit from multiple products, considering production constraints and resource limitations.
2. **Set Up Your Data:**
   - o List your variables (e.g., quantities of products) in a range of cells.
   - o Create a formula to calculate the objective (e.g., total profit) in a separate cell.
   - o Set up constraints (e.g., resource limits, production capacity) in additional cells.
3. **Access Solver:**
   - o Go to the Data tab and click on Solver.
4. **Set the Objective:**
   - o In the Solver Parameters dialog box, set the following:
     - ▪ **Set Objective:** Enter the cell with the objective formula (e.g., total profit).
     - ▪ **To:** Choose Max to maximize the value.
     - ▪ **By Changing Variable Cells:** Enter the range of cells with the variables to adjust (e.g., quantities of products).

5. **Add Constraints:**
   o Click Add to define constraints. For example, if the production capacity cannot exceed a certain amount, set the constraint accordingly.
6. **Solve the Problem:**
   o Click Solve. Solver will adjust the variable cells to maximize the objective while adhering to the constraints.

Practical Tips for Solver

- **Start Simple:** Begin with basic problems to understand how Solver works before tackling more complex scenarios.
- **Check Constraints:** Ensure all constraints are realistic and correctly defined.
- **Review Solutions:** Analyze Solver's solutions to ensure they make sense in your real-world context.

Real-World Example: Optimizing a Budget

Imagine you're managing a budget for multiple departments and need to allocate funds to maximize overall performance while staying within the total budget.

1. **Set Up Your Budget Data:**
   o List each department and their potential expenditures in a table.
   o Create a formula to calculate the total expenditure and the total benefit or performance score.
2. **Access Solver:**
   o Open Solver from the Data tab.
3. **Define the Objective:**
   o Set the objective to maximize the total benefit score.
4. **Adjust Variables:**
   o Specify the range of cells containing department expenditures as the variables to change.
5. **Add Constraints:**
   o Ensure the total expenditure does not exceed the allocated budget.
6. **Run Solver:**
   o Click Solve to find the optimal allocation of funds across departments to maximize performance.

Goal Seek and Solver are invaluable tools in your Excel arsenal, enabling you to tackle a wide range of data analysis challenges with precision and ease. By mastering these tools, you can move beyond basic calculations to perform sophisticated analyses that drive strategic decisions. Whether you're forecasting sales, optimizing resources, or managing budgets, these tools empower you to uncover insights and achieve your goals more effectively. Embrace the power of Goal Seek and Solver, and transform the way you approach data analysis in Excel 2024.

9.2 PERFORMING BASIC STATISTICAL ANALYSIS

Imagine you're sitting down with a massive pile of data. You know there's a story hidden within those numbers, but you need the right tools to uncover it. Excel's basic statistical analysis tools are like a magnifying glass, helping you to see patterns, trends, and insights that would otherwise remain hidden. These tools are essential for anyone looking to make informed decisions based on data, whether you're in business, research, or any other field. Let's explore how you can perform basic statistical analysis in Excel 2024, step by step.

Understanding Descriptive Statistics

Descriptive statistics are the foundation of data analysis. They summarize and describe the main features of a dataset in a meaningful way, providing a simple overview of the data's characteristics.

Mean, Median, and Mode

1. **Calculating the Mean (Average):**
   o The mean gives you the average value of your dataset.
   o Use the AVERAGE function:
   =AVERAGE(range)

For example, if your data is in cells A1 to A10, the formula would be =AVERAGE(A1:A10).

2. **Finding the Median:**
   o The median is the middle value when your data is sorted in ascending order.
   o Use the MEDIAN function:
   =MEDIAN(range)

For instance, =MEDIAN(A1:A10).

3. **Determining the Mode:**
   o The mode is the value that appears most frequently in your dataset.
   o Use the MODE.SNGL function:
   =MODE.SNGL(range)

For example, =MODE.SNGL(A1:A10).

Practical Tips for Descriptive Statistics

- **Clean Your Data:** Ensure there are no errors or outliers that could skew your results.
- **Use Named Ranges:** For clarity and ease of use, define named ranges for your data.

Measuring Dispersion

Dispersion metrics help you understand the spread or variability of your data, which is crucial for identifying the range and consistency.

Range, Variance, and Standard Deviation

1. **Calculating the Range:**
   - The range is the difference between the maximum and minimum values in your dataset.
   - Use the formula:
     =MAX(range) - MIN(range)

For instance, =MAX(A1:A10) - MIN(A1:A10).

2. **Finding the Variance:**
   - Variance measures how much the data points deviate from the mean.
   - Use the VAR.S function for a sample:
     =VAR.S(range)

For example, =VAR.S(A1:A10).

3. **Determining the Standard Deviation:**
   - Standard deviation provides a measure of the dispersion or spread of your data.
   - Use the STDEV.S function for a sample:
     =STDEV.S(range)

For instance, =STDEV.S(A1:A10).

Practical Tips for Measuring Dispersion

- **Consistency Check:** Compare the standard deviation with the mean to gauge the consistency of your data.
- **Visual Aids:** Use charts, such as histograms, to visually represent the dispersion of your data.

Using Excel's Data Analysis ToolPak

Excel's Data Analysis ToolPak provides an easy way to perform advanced statistical analyses.

Enabling the Data Analysis ToolPak

1. **Open Excel Options:**
   - Go to File > Options > Add-Ins.
2. **Manage Add-Ins:**
   - In the Manage box, select Excel Add-ins and click Go.
3. **Enable ToolPak:**
   - Check Analysis ToolPak and click OK.

Performing Basic Statistical Analysis with the ToolPak

1. **Access the ToolPak:**
   o Go to the Data tab and click on Data Analysis.
2. **Choose Descriptive Statistics:**
   o Select Descriptive Statistics from the list and click OK.
3. **Set Input Range:**
   o Specify the input range and select options such as Summary Statistics to generate a comprehensive report.

Real-World Example: Analyzing Sales Data

Imagine you have monthly sales data for a year, and you want to understand its characteristics.

1. **Calculate Descriptive Statistics:**
   o Use AVERAGE, MEDIAN, and MODE.SNGL to find central tendencies.
   o Use VAR.S and STDEV.S to measure variability.
2. **Generate a Summary Report:**
   o Use the Data Analysis ToolPak to produce a descriptive statistics summary, providing a snapshot of your sales performance.

Practical Tips for Using Data Analysis ToolPak

- **Explore Different Tools:** The ToolPak offers various statistical tools. Experiment with different analyses to deepen your understanding.
- **Check Assumptions:** Ensure your data meets the assumptions required for specific statistical tests.

Visualizing Statistical Data

Visualization helps in making sense of statistical data by providing an intuitive understanding of the data's behavior.

Creating Histograms

1. **Select Your Data:**
   o Highlight the range of your data.
2. **Insert Histogram:**
   o Go to the Insert tab, click on Insert Statistic Chart, and select Histogram.
3. **Customize the Chart:**
   o Adjust the bin range and labels to better represent your data.

Creating Box Plots

1. **Select Your Data:**
   - o Highlight the data range.
2. **Insert Box Plot:**
   - o Go to the Insert tab, select Insert Statistic Chart, and choose Box and Whisker.
3. **Interpret the Plot:**
   - o Analyze the quartiles, median, and potential outliers.

Performing basic statistical analysis in Excel equips you with the tools to derive meaningful insights from your data. By understanding central tendencies, measuring dispersion, and using advanced tools like the Data Analysis ToolPak, you can uncover patterns and trends that inform better decision-making. Visualization techniques like histograms and box plots further enhance your ability to interpret data intuitively. Embrace these statistical tools in Excel 2024, and transform your raw data into valuable information, empowering you to make informed and strategic decisions in your work.

9.3 INTRODUCTION TO WHAT-IF ANALYSIS

Imagine you're a pilot, navigating through a storm. You have various routes to take, and each decision could lead to a different outcome. This is where What-If Analysis in Excel comes into play—it's like having a flight simulator for your data, allowing you to explore different scenarios and outcomes without the risk. What-If Analysis helps you make informed decisions by showing you the potential impacts of changes to your data.

What-If Analysis: The Concept

What-If Analysis involves changing the values in your Excel formulas to see how those changes will affect the results. It's a powerful tool for exploring different scenarios and their outcomes, helping you to plan for various possibilities. Whether you're budgeting, forecasting, or conducting risk assessments, What-If Analysis can provide valuable insights.

Exploring What-If Analysis Tools

Excel offers several What-If Analysis tools, each designed to handle different types of scenarios. Let's explore these tools and how they can be used effectively.

Scenario Manager

Scenario Manager allows you to create and save different sets of values, or scenarios, and switch between them to see how they affect your spreadsheet.

1. **Setting Up Scenarios:**
   - Imagine you're preparing a budget. You want to see the impact of different expense levels on your overall budget.
   - Enter your initial data, such as expected revenues and expenses.
2. **Access Scenario Manager:**
   - Go to the Data tab, click on What-If Analysis, and select Scenario Manager.
3. **Create Scenarios:**
   - Click Add to create a new scenario. Name it (e.g., "Best Case"), select the cells that will change, and enter the new values.
   - Repeat this process for other scenarios (e.g., "Worst Case", "Most Likely Case").
4. **Switch Between Scenarios:**
   - In the Scenario Manager, select a scenario and click Show to see how the changes affect your budget.

Practical Tips for Using Scenario Manager

- **Plan Ahead:** Define the key variables and potential changes you want to explore.
- **Compare Outcomes:** Use Scenario Summary reports to compare different scenarios side by side.

Data Tables

Data Tables are useful for seeing how changing one or two variables affects multiple outcomes in your formulas. They're particularly handy for sensitivity analysis.

1. **Setting Up a One-Variable Data Table:**
   - Suppose you want to analyze how different interest rates affect loan payments.
   - Set up your formula (e.g., =PMT(rate, nper, pv)) with the interest rate in a separate cell.
2. **Create the Data Table:**
   - List different interest rates in a column.
   - Select the range, go to the Data tab, click What-If Analysis, and choose Data Table.
   - Enter the cell reference for the interest rate in the Column Input Cell box.
3. **Viewing the Results:**
   - Excel will populate the table with loan payments corresponding to each interest rate.
4. **Two-Variable Data Table:**
   - For more complex scenarios, you can use two variables (e.g., interest rates and loan terms).

Practical Tips for Using Data Tables

- **Keep It Simple:** Start with one-variable tables before progressing to two-variable tables.
- **Label Clearly:** Ensure your data tables are well-labeled to avoid confusion.

Goal Seek

Goal Seek is ideal for finding the input values needed to achieve a specific goal in your formula.

1. **Setting Up Goal Seek:**
   - o Let's say you want to determine the sales volume required to achieve a target profit.
   - o Set up your formula to calculate profit based on sales volume.
2. **Access Goal Seek:**
   - o Go to the Data tab, click What-If Analysis, and select Goal Seek.
3. **Define Your Goal:**
   - o Set the cell containing the profit formula as the Set cell.
   - o Enter the target profit as the To value.
   - o Select the cell containing the sales volume as the By changing cell.
4. **Execute Goal Seek:**
   - o Click OK, and Excel will adjust the sales volume to meet the target profit.

Practical Tips for Using Goal Seek

- **Precision Matters:** Ensure your initial data and formulas are accurate for reliable results.
- **Iterative Process:** Use Goal Seek iteratively to refine your targets and assumptions.

Real-World Example: Business Forecasting

Imagine you're a financial analyst forecasting next year's revenue. You can use What-If Analysis to explore various scenarios:

1. **Scenario Manager for Budget Planning:**
   - o Create scenarios for different revenue growth rates and expense increases.
   - o Switch between scenarios to see their impact on your net profit.
2. **Data Tables for Sensitivity Analysis:**
   - o Use a data table to analyze how changes in market conditions (e.g., price elasticity, customer acquisition rates) affect your revenue projections.
3. **Goal Seek for Target Setting:**
   - o Determine the sales targets needed to achieve a specific profit margin.

What-If Analysis in Excel is a powerful suite of tools that allows you to explore different scenarios and their outcomes. By using Scenario Manager, Data Tables, and Goal Seek, you can anticipate changes, plan effectively, and make informed decisions. These tools transform your approach to data analysis, turning uncertainty into clarity and strategic foresight. Embrace What-If Analysis in Excel 2024 to unlock the full potential of your data, ensuring you're always prepared for whatever challenges or opportunities come your way.

10. COLLABORATING AND SHARING WORKBOOKS

Imagine you're part of a dynamic team working on a major project. Everyone has insights and data to contribute, but coordinating these contributions can be a logistical nightmare. This is where Excel's collaboration and sharing features come into play, transforming what could be a chaotic process into a seamless, efficient workflow. In this chapter, we'll explore how Excel 2024 empowers you to collaborate and share workbooks effortlessly, ensuring that everyone stays on the same page and that your data remains secure and up-to-date.

Collaboration in Excel is about more than just sharing files. It's about working together in real-time, tracking changes, and integrating feedback without the headache of endless email chains and version confusion. With Excel 2024, you can invite colleagues to view and edit your workbooks, see who's making changes in real time, and communicate directly within the workbook to clarify points and make decisions quickly.

Sharing workbooks isn't just convenient—it's crucial for maintaining data integrity and fostering teamwork. By using Excel's built-in sharing features, you can control who has access to your data, what they can do with it, and how changes are tracked. Whether you're working with a small team on a local network or collaborating with partners across the globe via the cloud, Excel's sharing tools ensure that everyone is working with the latest information.

Imagine the possibilities: your sales team updating figures from different locations, a research team collaboratively analyzing data sets, or a project team synchronizing timelines and resources—all in real-time, with the confidence that everyone is seeing and contributing to the most current data. This chapter will guide you through the best practices for sharing and collaborating in Excel, helping you harness the full power of teamwork and ensuring your projects are completed efficiently and accurately. So, let's dive in and discover how Excel 2024 can make collaboration and sharing as smooth and productive as possible.

10.1 SHARING AND PROTECTING WORKBOOKS

Imagine you've just completed a critical workbook full of valuable data and insights. The next step is to share it with your team for their input and collaboration. But how do you ensure that the right people have access, and how do you protect your work from unauthorized changes? In this section, we'll explore how to share and protect workbooks in Excel 2024, ensuring a smooth and secure collaboration process.

Sharing Workbooks: Enhancing Team Collaboration

Sharing your workbook allows your team to view and edit the data, making collaboration seamless and efficient. Here's how to share your Excel workbook effectively.

Step-by-Step Guide to Sharing Workbooks

1. **Save Your Workbook to OneDrive or SharePoint:**
    o Before you can share a workbook, save it to a cloud location like OneDrive or SharePoint. Click on File, select Save As, and choose your OneDrive or SharePoint location.

2. **Share Your Workbook:**
   - o Once saved, click the Share button at the top right corner of the Excel window. This opens the sharing pane where you can invite others to collaborate.
   - o Enter the email addresses of the people you want to share the workbook with. You can also add a message to provide context or instructions.
   - o Set permissions by choosing whether the recipients can View or Edit the workbook. Click Send to share the link.
3. **Share via Link:**
   - o Alternatively, generate a shareable link by clicking Get a Link. You can then copy this link and send it via email or messaging apps.
   - o Customize the link permissions, specifying whether recipients can view or edit the document and setting an expiration date if necessary.

Practical Tips for Sharing Workbooks

- **Define Permissions Clearly:** Always set clear permissions to ensure that only the right people can edit the workbook.
- **Use Comments and Notes:** Encourage collaborators to use comments and notes within the workbook for clear communication.

Protecting Workbooks: Ensuring Data Integrity

Protecting your workbook is crucial to maintain data integrity and prevent unauthorized changes. Here's how to apply different levels of protection.

Step-by-Step Guide to Protecting Workbooks

1. **Protect Workbook Structure:**
   - o To protect the overall structure of your workbook, including the arrangement of sheets, click on File, then Info, and select Protect Workbook. Choose Encrypt with Password or Protect Structure.
   - o If you select Encrypt with Password, enter and confirm your password. This ensures that only users with the password can open the workbook.
   - o If you choose Protect Structure, you can restrict actions like adding, deleting, or moving sheets within the workbook.
2. **Protect Specific Worksheets:**
   - o To protect individual sheets, right-click on the sheet tab and select Protect Sheet. You can specify the actions that are allowed, such as selecting cells, formatting cells, or inserting rows.
   - o Enter a password to prevent others from unprotecting the sheet without your permission.
3. **Protect Cells and Ranges:**
   - o For more granular control, you can protect specific cells or ranges. Select the cells you want to protect, right-click, and choose Format Cells. Go to the Protection tab and check Locked.

o   Next, protect the sheet as described above to enforce these protections.

Practical Tips for Protecting Workbooks
- **Use Strong Passwords:** Always use strong, unique passwords to protect your workbooks and sheets.
- **Backup Your Workbook:** Regularly back up your workbook to prevent data loss in case of accidental overwriting or corruption.

Real-World Example: Collaborative Financial Planning
Imagine you're working on a financial planning workbook that requires input from multiple departments. Here's how you can share and protect it effectively:
1. **Saving and Sharing:**
   o   Save the workbook to OneDrive and share it with department heads, granting them editing permissions.
   o   Encourage them to use comments for suggestions and clarifications.
2. **Protecting the Structure:**
   o   Protect the workbook structure to prevent accidental rearrangement of sheets, ensuring that the workbook layout remains consistent.
3. **Protecting Sensitive Data:**
   o   Lock and protect cells containing sensitive data, such as salary information, so only authorized personnel can view or edit these cells.

Maintaining Version Control
Collaboration can sometimes lead to confusion about the most current version of a workbook. Excel provides tools to help maintain version control and track changes.

Using Version History
1. **Access Version History:**
   o   In your OneDrive or SharePoint, open the workbook and click on File, then Info, and select Version History.
2. **Review and Restore:**
   o   Browse through previous versions, view the changes made, and if necessary, restore an earlier version of the workbook.

Practical Tips for Version Control
- **Regularly Save and Sync:** Ensure everyone saves their changes regularly and syncs the workbook to maintain the most up-to-date version.
- **Communicate Changes:** Use comments or a shared log within the workbook to communicate significant changes to the team.

Sharing and protecting workbooks in Excel 2024 is essential for effective collaboration and data security. By understanding how to share workbooks, set appropriate permissions, and protect your data, you can ensure that your collaborative efforts are smooth and secure. With these tools and practices, you can confidently work together with your team, knowing that your data is safe and that everyone is working from the most current and accurate information. Embrace these strategies to enhance your Excel collaboration experience, making teamwork not only possible but also productive and secure.

10.2 TRACKING CHANGES AND COMMENTS

Imagine you're working on a complex Excel workbook with a team. Multiple people are making updates, suggestions, and changes. Keeping track of who did what and when can become a monumental task. That's where Excel's tracking changes and comments features come into play. These tools not only help you monitor modifications but also facilitate clear communication among team members. Let's dive into how you can effectively track changes and use comments to streamline your collaborative efforts in Excel 2024.

Tracking Changes: Keeping an Eye on Modifications

Tracking changes in Excel allows you to monitor edits made by different users. This is particularly useful in collaborative environments where maintaining an accurate record of changes is crucial.

Enabling Track Changes

1. **Save Your Workbook:**
   - Before enabling tracking, ensure your workbook is saved in a location accessible to all collaborators, preferably on OneDrive or SharePoint.
2. **Turn On Track Changes:**
   - Go to the Review tab on the ribbon.
   - Click on Track Changes and select Highlight Changes.
   - In the dialog box, check Track changes while editing. This also shares your workbook.
3. **Set Preferences:**
   - Specify the changes you want to track, such as Who, When, and Where.
   - You can choose to highlight changes made since your last save, all changes, or changes made by specific users.

Reviewing and Accepting Changes

1. **Review Changes:**
   - To review changes, go to the Review tab and click Track Changes, then select Accept/Reject Changes.
   - In the dialog box, specify the changes you want to review, and click OK.
2. **Accept or Reject:**
   - Excel will guide you through each change, allowing you to accept or reject it. This helps ensure that only the appropriate modifications are retained.

Practical Tips for Tracking Changes
- **Regular Reviews:** Regularly review changes to prevent a backlog of unreviewed modifications.
- **Clear Communication:** Use the comments feature alongside tracking changes to provide context for your edits.

Using Comments: Enhancing Communication

Comments in Excel allow team members to leave notes and feedback directly within the workbook. This feature is essential for providing explanations, suggestions, and clarifications without altering the data itself.

Adding Comments
1. **Select the Cell:**
   - Click on the cell where you want to add a comment.
2. **Insert Comment:**
   - Go to the Review tab and click on New Comment.
   - Type your comment in the box that appears. You can mention a specific user by typing @ followed by their name, ensuring they are notified.
3. **Post Comment:**
   - Click the Post button to save your comment. The cell will display a small indicator showing that it contains a comment.

Replying to Comments
1. **View Comments:**
   - To view comments, hover over the cell or go to the Review tab and click Show Comments. This opens the Comments pane, displaying all comments in the workbook.
2. **Reply to a Comment:**
   - In the Comments pane, find the comment you want to reply to and click Reply. Type your response and click Post.

Practical Tips for Using Comments
- **Be Specific:** Make your comments clear and specific to avoid misunderstandings.
- **Resolve Comments:** Once an issue is addressed, mark the comment as resolved to keep the workbook tidy.

Real-World Example: Collaborative Project Planning

Imagine you're managing a project where different team members are responsible for updating various parts of the project plan. Here's how tracking changes and comments can facilitate this process:
1. **Enable Track Changes:**
   - Save the project plan on OneDrive and enable track changes. This allows you to monitor who updates tasks, deadlines, and budgets.

2. **Add Comments for Clarity:**
   - As you review the updates, add comments to clarify any uncertainties or provide additional instructions. For example, if someone changes a deadline, you might comment, "Can we ensure this aligns with the marketing campaign schedule?"
3. **Review and Approve Changes:**
   - Regularly review the changes using the Accept/Reject Changes feature. This ensures all updates are intentional and agreed upon.
4. **Collaborate Efficiently:**
   - Use the comments pane to have threaded discussions about specific parts of the plan, resolving issues as they arise and maintaining a clear record of decisions.

Maintaining a Clean and Efficient Workbook

Regular use of tracking changes and comments can lead to a cluttered workbook if not managed properly. Here's how to maintain an organized workbook.

Cleaning Up After Review

1. **Accept/Reject All Changes:**
   - Once you've reviewed all changes, accept or reject them to finalize the modifications.
2. **Clear Resolved Comments:**
   - Remove or archive resolved comments to keep the workbook clean. You can mark comments as resolved or delete them if no longer needed.

Practical Tips for Maintaining Workbook Cleanliness

- **Set Review Intervals:** Schedule regular intervals for reviewing and cleaning up changes and comments.
- **Archive Decisions:** If a comment leads to a significant decision, consider summarizing it in a dedicated "Decisions" sheet within the workbook for future reference.

Tracking changes and using comments in Excel 2024 significantly enhance collaboration and communication within teams. By enabling track changes, you can keep a detailed record of all modifications, ensuring accountability and clarity. Comments provide a platform for discussions and feedback directly within the workbook, fostering a more interactive and collaborative environment. Implement these tools to maintain control over your collaborative projects, ensuring that every change is tracked, every comment is addressed, and your workbooks remain organized and efficient. Embrace these features to streamline your teamwork and make data-driven decisions with confidence.

10.3 COLLABORATING IN REAL-TIME

Imagine a bustling office where team members can update a shared workbook simultaneously, with everyone seeing changes in real-time. This seamless collaboration enhances productivity, reduces errors, and fosters a dynamic work environment. In Excel 2024, real-time collaboration is a powerful feature that transforms how teams work together. Let's explore how to effectively collaborate in real-time, ensuring your projects run smoothly and efficiently.

Setting Up Real-Time Collaboration

Real-time collaboration in Excel 2024 allows multiple users to edit a workbook simultaneously, with changes appearing instantly. This feature is especially useful for teams working on complex projects where timely updates are crucial.

Preparing Your Workbook for Real-Time Collaboration

1. **Save to OneDrive or SharePoint:**
   o   To enable real-time collaboration, save your workbook to a cloud location. Click on File, select Save As, and choose OneDrive or SharePoint.
2. **Share the Workbook:**
   o   Click the Share button at the top right corner of the Excel window. Enter the email addresses of the collaborators, set their permissions (either View or Edit), and click Send.

Collaborating in Real-Time: Step-by-Step Guide

1. **Start Collaborating:**
   o   Once the workbook is shared, your collaborators will receive an email with a link to the document. When they open it, you can all start working together.
2. **See Who's Editing:**
   o   In the upper-right corner of the workbook, you'll see icons representing each person currently editing. Hover over these icons to see their names.
3. **View Changes Instantly:**
   o   As you and your team edit the workbook, changes appear instantly. Each user's selection and cursor are highlighted, making it easy to see who is working on what.
4. **Add Comments for Clarity:**
   o   Use the Comments feature to leave notes or ask questions. This is especially useful for clarifying changes or providing additional context without altering the data.

Practical Tips for Effective Real-Time Collaboration

- **Communicate Clearly:** Use comments and in-cell notes to communicate with your team. This helps avoid misunderstandings and ensures everyone is on the same page.
- **Track Major Changes:** For significant updates, consider using the Track Changes feature to keep a record of what was altered and by whom.

- **Maintain Version Control:** Regularly save versions of your workbook to prevent data loss and provide restore points if needed.

Managing Conflicts

When multiple users edit the same cells or data ranges, conflicts can occur. Excel 2024 has tools to manage these conflicts smoothly.

Resolving Conflicts

1. **Conflict Notification:**
   - If a conflict arises, Excel will notify you with a message. The notification will explain the conflict and provide options to resolve it.
2. **Review Conflicts:**
   - Click on the notification to open the conflict resolution dialog. You can choose to keep your changes, accept the other user's changes, or merge the edits.
3. **Communicate with Collaborators:**
   - Use the Comments feature or an external communication tool to discuss conflicts and agree on the best resolution.

Practical Tips for Managing Conflicts

- **Set Collaboration Guidelines:** Establish clear guidelines for who edits which sections of the workbook to minimize conflicts.
- **Regular Check-Ins:** Schedule regular check-ins to review changes and address potential conflicts early.

Real-World Example: Collaborative Budget Planning

Consider a scenario where your team is collaboratively planning a budget for the upcoming fiscal year. Here's how real-time collaboration can streamline the process:

1. **Set Up the Workbook:**
   - Save the budget workbook to OneDrive and share it with your finance team, granting them editing permissions.
2. **Collaborate in Real-Time:**
   - As team members update their respective sections (e.g., department budgets), everyone sees the changes instantly. This ensures that all entries are up-to-date and no one works with outdated data.
3. **Use Comments for Clarifications:**
   - When someone adjusts a budget line item, they can add a comment explaining the change. This provides context and reduces the need for follow-up emails.
4. **Manage Conflicts:**
   - If two team members edit the same cell, they are notified of the conflict. They can then discuss the best solution and merge their edits accordingly.

Enhancing Productivity with Real-Time Collaboration

Real-time collaboration not only enhances productivity but also improves accuracy and team cohesion. Here are some additional tips to make the most of this feature:

- **Stay Synchronized:** Regularly synchronize your work to ensure everyone is working with the latest data.

- **Use Named Ranges:** Named ranges make it easier to refer to specific data sets, reducing confusion during collaborative editing.

- **Leverage Conditional Formatting:** Use conditional formatting to highlight important data changes, helping team members quickly identify key updates.

Real-time collaboration in Excel 2024 revolutionizes how teams work together. By enabling multiple users to edit the same workbook simultaneously, it fosters a dynamic and efficient work environment. Clear communication, effective conflict management, and strategic use of comments and notes ensure that your team can collaborate seamlessly. Embrace these features to enhance your collaborative projects, ensuring that your work is always accurate, up-to-date, and well-coordinated. With real-time collaboration, Excel becomes not just a tool for data entry and analysis, but a platform for teamwork and shared success.

11. ADVANCED EXCEL FEATURES FOR BEGINNERS

Imagine stepping into a world where Excel transforms from a simple spreadsheet tool into a powerhouse of advanced features that can streamline your workflows, automate repetitive tasks, and unlock deeper insights from your data. While Excel is renowned for its basic functions, it also boasts a suite of advanced features that can significantly enhance your productivity and analytical capabilities. In this chapter, we'll explore these powerful tools, designed to elevate your skills even if you're just starting out.

Advanced features in Excel might seem daunting at first glance, but they are incredibly accessible and immensely rewarding once you start using them. These tools are not just for experts; they are designed to help beginners become more efficient and proficient. From automating tasks with macros to utilizing powerful add-ins like Power Query and Power Pivot, Excel offers a range of functionalities that can simplify complex processes and provide new insights into your data.

Consider the possibilities: automating your monthly reports with a few clicks, transforming and combining data from various sources effortlessly, or creating dynamic dashboards that provide real-time insights. These advanced features can save you hours of work and enable you to focus on what really matters—analyzing and interpreting your data.

In this chapter, we'll demystify these advanced tools with clear, step-by-step instructions and practical tips. You'll learn how to harness the power of macros to automate repetitive tasks, explore the capabilities of Excel add-ins to extend your functionality, and discover how Power Query and Power Pivot can revolutionize the way you handle large datasets.

By the end of this chapter, you'll not only be familiar with these advanced features but also confident in applying them to your daily tasks. Excel's advanced tools are within your reach, ready to transform your data handling and analysis processes. Let's embark on this journey to unlock the full potential of Excel, making your work more efficient, insightful, and impactful.

11.1 INTRODUCTION TO MACROS

Imagine you could automate repetitive tasks in Excel, saving hours of manual work and reducing the chance of errors. This is the magic of macros, one of Excel's most powerful features. Macros are like scripts that automate routine tasks, allowing you to focus on more important aspects of your work. Whether you're a beginner or just starting to explore Excel's advanced capabilities, understanding macros can significantly boost your productivity.

What Are Macros?

Macros are sequences of instructions that automate tasks you frequently perform in Excel. Think of them as a set of actions recorded in a specific order, which can be played back anytime you need to repeat the task. They are particularly useful for tasks that require multiple steps, such as formatting data, creating reports, or applying consistent formulas across different sheets.

The Basics of Recording Macros

The easiest way to create a macro is to record it. Excel's macro recorder captures your actions and converts them into VBA (Visual Basic for Applications) code, which you can run with a single click.

Step-by-Step Guide to Recording a Macro

1. **Prepare Your Workbook:**
   - Open the workbook where you want to record the macro. Ensure you have all the data and tools you need to complete the task.

2. **Start Recording:**
   - Go to the View tab on the ribbon, click on Macros, and select Record Macro.
   - In the dialog box, give your macro a name (avoid spaces and special characters), assign a shortcut key if desired, and choose where to store the macro (usually in This Workbook).

3. **Perform the Task:**
   - Carry out the actions you want to automate. For example, if you want to format a range of cells, apply the desired formatting as you normally would.

4. **Stop Recording:**
   - Once you've completed the task, go back to the View tab, click on Macros, and select Stop Recording.

Running a Macro

After recording a macro, you can run it anytime to perform the automated task.

1. **Run from the Ribbon:**
   - Go to the View tab, click Macros, and select View Macros.
   - In the dialog box, choose the macro you want to run and click Run.

2. **Use a Shortcut Key:**
   - If you assigned a shortcut key during the recording, simply press that key combination to execute the macro.

Editing Macros

Sometimes, you may need to tweak your macros to refine their functionality. This involves editing the VBA code that Excel generated.

1. **Access the VBA Editor:**
   - Go to the View tab, click Macros, select View Macros, choose your macro, and click Edit.
   - This opens the VBA editor, where you can see and edit the code.
2. **Understand Basic VBA:**
   - While you don't need to be a programming expert, understanding basic VBA syntax can help you make minor adjustments. For example, changing cell references or adding new actions.

Practical Tips for Using Macros

- **Keep It Simple:** Start with simple tasks and gradually build more complex macros as you become comfortable.
- **Test Thoroughly:** Always test your macros on a copy of your data to ensure they work correctly without risking your actual data.
- **Document Your Macros:** Add comments to your VBA code to remind yourself or inform others of what each part of the macro does.

Real-World Example: Automating a Monthly Report

Imagine you need to generate a monthly sales report. This involves formatting the data, applying specific formulas, and creating a summary table. Here's how a macro can automate this process:

1. **Record the Macro:**
   - Open your sales data workbook and start recording a macro named "MonthlyReport".
   - Format the data, apply necessary formulas, and create the summary table.
   - Stop the recording once the task is complete.
2. **Run the Macro Monthly:**
   - Each month, simply run the "MonthlyReport" macro to automatically perform all these actions, saving you time and ensuring consistency.

Advanced Macro Techniques

As you become more comfortable with macros, you can explore advanced techniques such as:

- **Using Conditional Statements:**
  - Add logic to your macros to handle different scenarios. For example, applying different formats based on the value of a cell.
- **Looping Through Data:**
  - Create loops to perform actions on multiple sheets or data ranges. For example, applying a formula to all sheets in a workbook.

- **Creating User Forms:**
  - o Design custom dialog boxes to interact with users, making your macros more flexible and user-friendly.

Macros are a powerful tool in Excel 2024 that can transform how you work by automating repetitive tasks, ensuring consistency, and reducing errors. By learning how to record, run, and edit macros, you can streamline your workflows and focus on more strategic activities. Start with simple tasks, gradually explore more advanced techniques, and you'll soon find that macros are an invaluable part of your Excel toolkit. Embrace this feature to enhance your productivity and unlock new possibilities in your data management and analysis processes.

11.2 USING EXCEL ADD-INS

Imagine you're a chef, and your kitchen is stocked with every gadget imaginable. Some you use daily, others only for special dishes. Excel add-ins are like those specialized kitchen tools—they can enhance your productivity and enable you to perform tasks that would be difficult or time-consuming otherwise. In this section, we'll explore how to use Excel add-ins, powerful extensions that add extra functionality to your spreadsheets.

What Are Excel Add-Ins?

Excel add-ins are programs that provide additional features and tools beyond the standard Excel capabilities. They can help with a variety of tasks, from advanced data analysis to custom visualizations and enhanced automation. Whether you're working with complex datasets or looking to streamline your workflows, there's likely an add-in that can help.

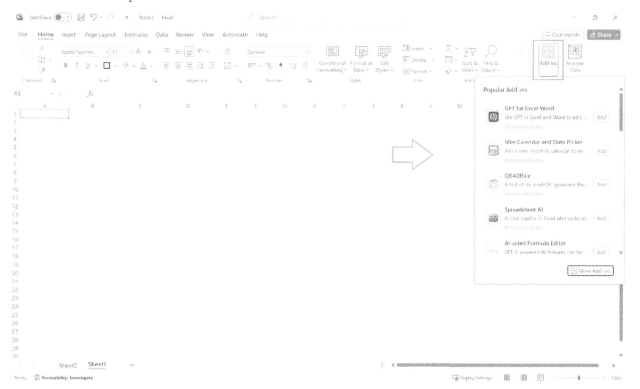

Installing and Managing Add-Ins

Step-by-Step Guide to Installing Add-Ins

1. **Open Excel Add-Ins:**
   - Start Excel and go to the Insert tab. Click on Get Add-ins to open the Office Add-ins store.
2. **Search for Add-Ins:**
   - In the Add-ins window, you can browse by category or use the search bar to find specific add-ins. For example, if you're looking for data analysis tools, you might search for "Analysis ToolPak."
3. **Install the Add-In:**
   - Once you find an add-in you want to use, click Add to install it. Follow any additional prompts to complete the installation.
4. **Manage Your Add-Ins:**
   - To manage your installed add-ins, go to File > Options > Add-Ins. Here, you can enable or disable add-ins as needed.

Using Popular Excel Add-Ins

Analysis ToolPak

The Analysis ToolPak is an essential add-in for performing complex statistical and engineering analysis. It provides functions for data analysis that are not available in the standard Excel package.

1. **Activate Analysis ToolPak:**
   - Go to File > Options > Add-Ins. In the Manage box, select Excel Add-ins and click Go. Check the Analysis ToolPak box and click OK.
2. **Accessing Analysis ToolPak:**
   - Once activated, you can access it from the Data tab under Data Analysis.
3. **Using Analysis ToolPak:**
   - To perform a specific analysis, click Data Analysis, choose the desired tool (e.g., Regression, Descriptive Statistics), and fill out the required input ranges and options.

Power Query

Power Query is a powerful tool for data connection, transformation, and combination. It simplifies the process of importing and cleaning data from various sources.

1. **Access Power Query:**
   - Go to the Data tab and click on Get Data. This opens the Power Query Editor.
2. **Importing Data:**
   - Choose your data source (e.g., Excel file, CSV, web page). Follow the prompts to connect to your data.

3. **Transforming Data:**
   o Use the Power Query Editor to clean and transform your data. You can remove duplicates, split columns, and merge tables with a few clicks.

4. **Loading Data:**
   o Once your data is ready, click Close & Load to import it into Excel.

Power Pivot

Power Pivot is another powerful add-in for data modeling and analysis. It allows you to create complex data models and perform calculations using DAX (Data Analysis Expressions).

1. **Activate Power Pivot:**
   o Go to File > Options > Add-Ins. In the Manage box, select COM Add-ins and click Go. Check the Microsoft Power Pivot for Excel box and click OK.

2. **Creating a Data Model:**
   o Go to the Power Pivot tab and click Manage. This opens the Power Pivot window where you can create your data model.

3. **Adding Data to Power Pivot:**
   o Import data into Power Pivot from various sources, and create relationships between tables to build your data model.

4. **Using DAX for Calculations:**
   o Use DAX functions to perform complex calculations and aggregations. For example, you can create measures to calculate sales growth or average sales per region.

Practical Tips for Using Add-Ins

- **Start Simple:** Begin with one or two add-ins that are most relevant to your work. Get comfortable with their features before exploring others.
- **Regular Updates:** Ensure your add-ins are updated to the latest version for optimal performance and security.
- **Backup Data:** Before performing major transformations or analyses, always back up your data to prevent accidental loss.

Real-World Example: Streamlining Data Analysis

Imagine you're an analyst responsible for preparing monthly sales reports. By using Excel add-ins, you can streamline the process:

1. **Use Power Query to Import Data:**
   o Import sales data from various sources, such as databases and CSV files, into Excel. Clean and transform the data to ensure consistency.

2. **Analyze with Analysis ToolPak:**
   o Use the Analysis ToolPak to perform statistical analyses, such as calculating the mean, median, and standard deviation of sales figures.

3. **Model Data with Power Pivot:**
   - Create a data model in Power Pivot to analyze sales trends across different regions and product categories. Use DAX to create measures for key performance indicators (KPIs).
4. **Automate with Macros:**
   - Automate repetitive tasks, such as formatting reports and updating charts, with macros to save time and reduce errors.

Excel add-ins are like powerful extensions that significantly enhance the functionality of your spreadsheets. By leveraging add-ins such as the Analysis ToolPak, Power Query, and Power Pivot, you can perform advanced data analysis, streamline data preparation, and build sophisticated data models. These tools transform Excel from a basic spreadsheet application into a comprehensive platform for data-driven decision-making. Start exploring these add-ins today to unlock new levels of productivity and insight in your work. With a bit of practice, you'll find that these advanced features are not only accessible but also incredibly valuable for tackling complex data challenges.

11.3 EXPLORING POWER QUERY AND POWER PIVOT

Imagine you're an architect, meticulously designing a complex structure. Your tools must be precise, efficient, and capable of handling intricate details. In the world of data, Power Query and Power Pivot are those advanced tools in Excel 2024 that empower you to handle complex data transformations and analysis with precision and ease. These features go beyond basic functions, enabling you to connect, transform, and analyze vast amounts of data seamlessly.

Understanding Power Query

Power Query is Excel's powerful data connection technology that allows you to discover, connect, combine, and refine data across a wide variety of sources. It simplifies data preparation, making it accessible even for beginners.

Step-by-Step Guide to Using Power Query
1. **Accessing Power Query:**
   - Open Excel and go to the Data tab. Click on Get Data to see a variety of data sources you can connect to, such as databases, online services, and files.
2. **Connecting to Data:**
   - Select your data source. For example, choose From File > From Excel Workbook to import data from another Excel file.
   - Navigate to the file and click Import.
3. **Transforming Data:**
   - Once the data is loaded into the Power Query Editor, you can clean and transform it. Common transformations include removing duplicates, filtering rows, splitting columns, and changing data types.

o   Use the ribbon in the Power Query Editor to apply these transformations. Each step is recorded and can be modified or deleted.

4. **Loading Data into Excel:**
   o   After transforming your data, click Close & Load to load the data into Excel. You can choose to load it into a new worksheet or an existing one.

Practical Tips for Power Query

- **Keep Transformations Simple:** Start with basic transformations and gradually add complexity as you become more comfortable.
- **Save Steps:** Each transformation step is saved in the query, making it easy to modify or replicate the process later.

Real-World Example: Cleaning Sales Data

Imagine you receive monthly sales data from different regions, often in inconsistent formats. Power Query can streamline this process:

1. **Import Data from Multiple Files:**
   o   Use Power Query to import sales data from multiple Excel files.
2. **Combine and Clean Data:**
   o   Merge these files into a single table, remove duplicates, and standardize formats.
3. **Load Clean Data:**
   o   Load the cleaned data into Excel, ready for analysis.

Understanding Power Pivot

Power Pivot is Excel's data modeling technology that allows you to create complex data models, integrate large datasets, and perform powerful calculations using Data Analysis Expressions (DAX).

Step-by-Step Guide to Using Power Pivot

1. **Activating Power Pivot:**
   o   Go to File > Options > Add-Ins. In the Manage box, select COM Add-ins and click Go. Check Microsoft Power Pivot for Excel and click OK.
2. **Importing Data into Power Pivot:**
   o   Go to the Power Pivot tab and click Manage to open the Power Pivot window.
   o   Click Get External Data to import data from various sources, such as databases or other Excel files.
3. **Creating Relationships:**
   o   In the Power Pivot window, create relationships between different tables to integrate your data. Drag fields to connect related data across tables, enabling advanced analysis.

4. **Using DAX for Advanced Calculations:**
   o Use DAX to create measures and calculated columns. For example, to calculate total sales, use a formula like:

   Total Sales = SUM(Sales[Amount])

5. **Building Your Data Model:**
   o Organize your data into a coherent model, making it easy to create PivotTables and PivotCharts in Excel.

Practical Tips for Power Pivot

- **Understand Relationships:** Properly defined relationships between tables are crucial for accurate data modeling.
- **Learn Basic DAX:** Familiarize yourself with basic DAX functions to perform powerful calculations and analyses.

Real-World Example: Financial Reporting

Suppose you need to create a comprehensive financial report integrating data from multiple sources, such as sales, expenses, and forecasts:

1. **Import Data:**
   o Use Power Pivot to import data from different financial systems.

2. **Create Relationships:**
   o Establish relationships between tables, such as linking sales data with expense data.

3. **Analyze with DAX:**
   o Use DAX to calculate key metrics, such as profit margins, growth rates, and forecasted revenue.

4. **Build Interactive Reports:**
   o Create interactive PivotTables and PivotCharts to visualize financial performance and trends.

Power Query and Power Pivot are transformative tools in Excel 2024, enabling you to handle complex data tasks with ease and precision. Power Query simplifies the process of connecting, cleaning, and transforming data, making it accessible even for beginners. Power Pivot takes data analysis to the next level, allowing you to create sophisticated data models and perform advanced calculations. By mastering these tools, you can streamline data preparation, integrate diverse datasets, and unlock deeper insights, making your data work harder for you. Embrace these advanced features to enhance your productivity and analytical capabilities, turning raw data into actionable intelligence with ease.

APPENDICES

As we conclude our journey through the expansive world of Excel, it's important to recognize that the learning doesn't stop here. The appendices in this guide serve as a treasure trove of additional resources, quick reference guides, and troubleshooting tips designed to support you long after you've mastered the basics. Think of the appendices as your personal toolkit, ready to assist you whenever you encounter challenges or need a refresher on specific topics.

The appendices are crafted to be your go-to resource for quick answers and deeper dives into Excel's functionalities. Whether you're facing a complex formula error, need to recall a specific keyboard shortcut, or seek advanced techniques for data analysis, this section has you covered. It's a comprehensive support system that complements the main chapters, ensuring you have all the tools necessary to excel in your Excel endeavors. Imagine working on a crucial project and hitting a roadblock—perhaps an unfamiliar error message or a forgotten function. Instead of sifting through endless online forums or tutorials, you can turn to the appendices. Here, you'll find clear, concise solutions and explanations that can get you back on track swiftly. This section is designed to be user-friendly, with organized content that makes finding information straightforward and intuitive.

In addition to troubleshooting and quick references, the appendices also provide further reading and resources for those eager to deepen their expertise. Links to online courses, recommended books, and helpful websites will guide your continued learning, ensuring you stay ahead of the curve in your Excel proficiency.

The journey to mastering Excel is ongoing, and with the appendices, you have a reliable companion to assist you along the way. Dive into these resources whenever you need support, clarity, or inspiration. Remember, the goal is not just to use Excel, but to wield it with confidence and skill, transforming data into actionable insights with ease. The appendices are here to ensure that you can do just that, empowering you to tackle any spreadsheet challenge that comes your way.

A. QUICK REFERENCE GUIDES

Imagine you're in the middle of an intense project, juggling multiple tasks and deadlines. Suddenly, you hit a roadblock—an Excel function you can't quite remember, a formula that's giving you trouble, or a formatting issue you can't resolve. This is where quick reference guides become invaluable. These guides are designed to provide immediate answers and refresh your memory, ensuring you can maintain your workflow without unnecessary interruptions.

Navigating the Quick Reference Guides

The Quick Reference Guides in this appendix are your go-to resources for instant help with Excel's most frequently used features and functions. Organized for easy access, they cover everything from basic shortcuts to advanced formulas, offering clear and concise instructions that you can apply on the fly.

Essential Keyboard Shortcuts

Mastering keyboard shortcuts can significantly enhance your efficiency. Here are some of the most useful shortcuts that can save you time and streamline your workflow:

- **Ctrl + C**: Copy
- **Ctrl + V**: Paste
- **Ctrl + Z**: Undo
- **Ctrl + Y**: Redo
- **Ctrl + F**: Find
- **Ctrl + H**: Replace
- **Ctrl + A**: Select All
- **Ctrl + S**: Save
- **Ctrl + P**: Print
- **Alt + Enter**: Insert a line break within a cell
- **F2**: Edit the active cell
- **F4**: Repeat the last action

Basic Formulas and Functions

Excel's power lies in its ability to perform complex calculations with ease. Here are some fundamental formulas and functions you should always have at your fingertips:

1. **SUM**: Adds a range of cells.
   =SUM(A1:A10)
2. **AVERAGE**: Calculates the average of a range of cells.
   =AVERAGE(B1:B10)
3. **COUNT**: Counts the number of cells that contain numbers.
   =COUNT(C1:C10)
4. **IF**: Performs a logical test and returns one value for a TRUE result and another for a FALSE result.
   =IF(D1>100, "High", "Low")
5. **VLOOKUP**: Searches for a value in the first column of a table and returns a value in the same row from a specified column.
   =VLOOKUP(E1, A1:B10, 2, FALSE)

Formatting Tips

Proper formatting can make your data more readable and professional. Here are some quick tips to enhance your spreadsheets:

- **Bold**: Highlight the text and press **Ctrl + B**.
- **Italics**: Highlight the text and press **Ctrl + I**.
- **Underline**: Highlight the text and press **Ctrl + U**.
- **Cell Colors**: Select the cells, go to the Home tab, and choose a color from the Fill Color dropdown.
- **Borders**: Select the cells, go to the Home tab, and click the Borders button to choose a border style.

Data Analysis Tools

For more advanced data handling, these tools are essential:

1. **PivotTables**: Summarize large datasets and analyze data from different perspectives.
   - Select your data range, go to the Insert tab, and click PivotTable.
2. **Conditional Formatting**: Automatically format cells based on their values.
   - Select your range, go to the Home tab, click Conditional Formatting, and choose a rule.
3. **Data Validation**: Restrict the type of data entered in cells.
   - Select your range, go to the Data tab, and click Data Validation.

Troubleshooting Common Issues

Even seasoned Excel users encounter problems. Here's how to solve some common issues:

1. **#VALUE! Error**: This occurs when the formula includes cells with different data types.
   - Check your formula to ensure it only includes numerical data or compatible data types.
2. **Circular Reference**: This happens when a formula refers back to its own cell.
   - Use the Formulas tab to trace and correct the circular reference.
3. **Excel Freezing**: If Excel becomes unresponsive, try closing other applications to free up resources or update Excel to the latest version.

Real-World Example: Monthly Sales Report

Imagine you're preparing a monthly sales report. Here's how quick reference guides can assist:

1. **Summing Sales Data**:
   - Use the SUM function to calculate total sales:
   =SUM(F2:F30)
2. **Average Sales**:
   - Calculate average sales per day with the AVERAGE function:
   =AVERAGE(F2:F30)
3. **Formatting for Readability**:
   - Bold the headers for clarity:
     - Select the header row and press **Ctrl + B**.
   - Apply conditional formatting to highlight sales exceeding a target:
     - Select the sales data range, go to Conditional Formatting, and choose Highlight Cells Rules > Greater Than.
4. **Creating a PivotTable**:
   - Summarize sales by region:
     - Select your data range, go to Insert > PivotTable, and arrange fields to show sales by region.

Quick reference guides are your secret weapon for efficient and effective Excel use. They provide immediate solutions and refresh your knowledge on key functions, formulas, and features, ensuring you can tackle any task with confidence. Keep this guide handy, and you'll find that navigating Excel's vast capabilities becomes a smoother, more intuitive process. With these tools at your disposal, you can maintain your workflow, reduce errors, and elevate your productivity, making every project more manageable and successful.

B. COMMON EXCEL ERRORS AND TROUBLESHOOTING

Imagine you're deep into a critical Excel project, making great progress, when suddenly you encounter an error. Frustrating, isn't it? Errors in Excel are like unexpected roadblocks, but understanding common errors and knowing how to troubleshoot them can help you quickly get back on track. Let's delve into some of the most frequent errors in Excel and explore effective ways to resolve them, ensuring your workflow remains smooth and efficient.

Understanding and Resolving Common Excel Errors

Excel errors can seem daunting, but each one provides clues to what went wrong. Here are some of the most common errors you might encounter and practical steps to fix them.

The #VALUE! Error

The #VALUE! error typically occurs when a formula includes cells with different data types, such as mixing text and numbers.

Step-by-Step Troubleshooting

1. **Identify the Cause:**
   - Look at the formula causing the error. Check each cell reference to ensure they contain the expected data types (e.g., numbers for arithmetic operations).
2. **Correct Data Types:**
   - If a cell contains text that should be a number, convert it. Click the cell, and use the VALUE function:
   =VALUE(A1)
3. **Simplify Formulas:**
   - Break down complex formulas into smaller parts to identify where the error is occurring.

Real-World Example

Imagine you're calculating the total cost of items in column B, but some cells contain text instead of numbers. The formula =SUM(B1:B10) might result in a #VALUE! error. To fix this, ensure all cells in column B are numeric, or use:
   =SUM(IF(ISNUMBER(B1:B10), B1:B10, 0))

The #REF! Error

The #REF! error appears when a formula refers to a cell that is not valid, often because it was deleted or the reference is out of bounds.

Step-by-Step Troubleshooting

1. **Find the Broken Reference:**
   o   Click on the cell with the #REF! error to see which part of the formula is causing the problem.
2. **Restore or Adjust the Reference:**
   o   If a cell or range was deleted, you can undo the deletion (if recent) or adjust the formula to reference the correct cells.
3. **Use Absolute References:**
   o   To prevent this in the future, use absolute references where appropriate (e.g., A1 instead of A1).

Real-World Example

Suppose you have a formula =A1+B1 and you delete column B. The formula changes to =A1+#REF!. To fix this, update the formula to reference the correct cells or restore the deleted column.

The #DIV/0! Error

This error occurs when a formula attempts to divide by zero or an empty cell.

Step-by-Step Troubleshooting

1. **Check for Zero or Empty Cells:**
   o   Identify the cells involved in the division. Ensure the denominator is not zero or empty.
2. **Add Error Handling:**
   o   Use the IFERROR function to handle this gracefully:
   =IFERROR(A1/B1, "Error: Division by zero")
3. **Prevent Zero Values:**
   o   Use data validation to prevent users from entering zero in the denominator cells.

Real-World Example

If you have a formula =A1/B1 and B1 is zero, the result will be #DIV/0!. To handle this, you can use:
   =IF(B1=0, "Error: Division by zero", A1/B1)

The #NAME? Error

The #NAME? error suggests Excel doesn't recognize part of your formula, often due to a typo in function names or named ranges.

Step-by-Step Troubleshooting

1. **Check for Typos:**
   - Verify that all function names are spelled correctly. Excel functions are case-insensitive but must be spelled correctly.
2. **Ensure Named Ranges Exist:**
   - If using named ranges, make sure they are defined. Go to Formulas > Name Manager to review them.
3. **Verify Add-Ins:**
   - Ensure any custom functions or add-ins required by the formula are installed and enabled.

Real-World Example

If you type =SMU(A1:A10) instead of =SUM(A1:A10), Excel will return a #NAME? error. Correct the typo to fix this.

The Circular Reference Error

A circular reference occurs when a formula refers back to its own cell, causing an endless loop.

Step-by-Step Troubleshooting

1. **Identify the Circular Reference:**
   - Excel typically notifies you about circular references. Click the warning to locate the cell involved.
2. **Break the Loop:**
   - Adjust the formula to eliminate the self-reference. Sometimes, using an intermediate calculation in another cell helps.
3. **Use Iterative Calculation:**
   - If a circular reference is intentional (e.g., for iterative calculations), enable iterative calculations in File > Options > Formulas.

Real-World Example

If cell A1 has the formula =A1+1, Excel will alert you to the circular reference. To resolve this, use a different cell for the iterative part of the calculation.

Practical Tips for Troubleshooting

- **Use Excel's Error Checking Tool:**
  - Excel's built-in error checking tool can guide you through resolving common errors. Find it under Formulas > Error Checking.

- **Break Down Formulas:**
  - o Simplify complex formulas into smaller parts to isolate and fix errors.
- **Regularly Save Your Work:**
  - o Frequent saving prevents data loss during troubleshooting.

Encountering errors in Excel can be frustrating, but understanding common errors and how to troubleshoot them effectively turns these challenges into minor detours rather than roadblocks. By learning to interpret error messages and applying practical solutions, you can quickly resolve issues and maintain a smooth workflow. Keep this guide handy as a quick reference, and remember that each error is an opportunity to deepen your Excel expertise. With practice, you'll find that troubleshooting becomes second nature, allowing you to navigate Excel with confidence and efficiency.

C. ADDITIONAL RESOURCES AND FURTHER READING

As you journey deeper into the world of Excel, you might find yourself eager to explore beyond the confines of this book. There's a vast ocean of resources waiting to enhance your understanding, introduce you to advanced techniques, and keep you updated with the latest Excel developments. In this section, we'll explore various resources and further reading materials that can propel your Excel skills to the next level. Whether you're looking for detailed tutorials, expert advice, or community support, these resources have you covered.

Online Learning Platforms

Online learning platforms offer a structured and flexible way to improve your Excel skills at your own pace. Here are a few that stand out:

Coursera

Coursera partners with top universities and organizations to offer courses that range from beginner to advanced levels. Courses like "Excel Skills for Business" by Macquarie University are highly rated and comprehensive.

1. **Step-by-Step Learning:**
   - o Courses are designed to build your skills progressively, with each module focusing on specific aspects of Excel.
2. **Interactive Content:**
   - o Engage with video tutorials, quizzes, and peer discussions to reinforce learning.

LinkedIn Learning

Formerly known as Lynda.com, LinkedIn Learning offers a wide range of Excel courses tailored to different skill levels and professional needs.

1. **Real-World Applications:**
   - o Courses are designed by industry professionals, ensuring practical, real-world relevance.
2. **Certifications:**
   - o Earn certificates of completion that you can showcase on your LinkedIn profile.

Books and E-Books

For those who prefer a more traditional approach to learning, books and e-books provide in-depth coverage of Excel topics. Here are a few recommendations:

"Excel 2024 Bible" by John Walkenbach

This comprehensive guide covers everything from basic functions to advanced techniques, making it a valuable resource for users at all levels.

1. **Detailed Explanations:**
   - Each topic is explained thoroughly, with practical examples to illustrate complex concepts.
2. **Reference Sections:**
   - Includes quick reference sections for formulas, functions, and shortcuts.

"Data Analysis with Microsoft Excel" by Kenneth N. Berk and Patrick Carey

This book focuses on data analysis techniques, making it perfect for users looking to leverage Excel's analytical capabilities.

1. **Practical Focus:**
   - Emphasizes practical applications of data analysis in business and research.
2. **Step-by-Step Instructions:**
   - Detailed, step-by-step instructions ensure you can follow along and apply what you learn.

Online Communities and Forums

Engaging with online communities and forums can provide support, insights, and solutions from fellow Excel enthusiasts and experts. These platforms are invaluable for troubleshooting, sharing knowledge, and staying updated with the latest trends.

Reddit (r/excel)

Reddit's Excel community is a vibrant space where users post questions, share tips, and discuss various Excel topics.

1. **Real-Time Assistance:**
   - Get answers to your questions quickly from a diverse group of Excel users.
2. **Resource Sharing:**
   - Discover tutorials, templates, and tools shared by community members.

Stack Overflow

A well-known platform for programmers, Stack Overflow also has a large community of Excel users.

1. **Problem-Solving Focus:**
   - Ideal for finding solutions to specific problems or learning advanced techniques.
2. **Peer Support:**
   - Engage with experienced Excel users who offer insights and solutions.

Blogs and Websites

Several blogs and websites offer tutorials, tips, and updates on Excel. These resources are great for continuous learning and staying informed about new features and best practices.

ExcelJet

ExcelJet provides concise, practical tutorials and tips to help you get more out of Excel.

1. **Focused Content:**
   o   Tutorials are short and focused on specific functions or techniques, making them easy to digest.
2. **Templates and Tools:**
   o   Access a variety of templates and tools to enhance your Excel projects.

Chandoo.org

Run by MVP Chandoo, this site offers a wealth of resources, including tutorials, templates, and a community forum.

1. **Comprehensive Tutorials:**
   o   Covers a wide range of topics from basic to advanced, with clear, step-by-step instructions.
2. **Interactive Learning:**
   o   Participate in forums and webinars to interact with other learners and experts.

Further Reading and Continuous Learning

Excel is constantly evolving, and staying updated with new features and techniques is crucial for maintaining your proficiency. Here are some strategies to ensure continuous learning:

1. **Subscribe to Newsletters:**
   o   Sign up for newsletters from Excel blogs and websites to receive regular updates, tips, and tutorials.
2. **Join Webinars and Workshops:**
   o   Participate in webinars and workshops offered by Excel experts to learn about the latest features and advanced techniques.
3. **Engage with Professional Networks:**
   o   Join professional networks and associations related to data analysis and business intelligence to connect with like-minded professionals and stay informed about industry trends.

Real-World Example: Enhancing Skills for a Data Analyst Role

Imagine you're a data analyst looking to enhance your Excel skills to improve your job performance. Here's how you can leverage the resources mentioned above:

1. **Online Learning:**
   o   Enroll in a Coursera course on advanced Excel techniques to build a strong foundation.
2. **Books:**
   o   Use the "Excel 2024 Bible" as a reference guide to explore advanced functions and features.

3. **Online Communities:**
   - o   Join Reddit's Excel community to ask questions and learn from others' experiences.
4. **Websites and Blogs:**
   - o   Follow ExcelJet and Chandoo.org for regular tips and tutorials to keep your skills sharp.
5. **Continuous Learning:**
   - o   Subscribe to newsletters and participate in webinars to stay updated with the latest Excel advancements.

Embarking on the journey to master Excel is both exciting and rewarding. The additional resources and further reading materials highlighted in this section are designed to support your continuous learning and professional growth. By leveraging these tools and communities, you can enhance your proficiency, stay updated with the latest developments, and connect with fellow Excel enthusiasts. Remember, learning Excel is an ongoing process, and these resources will ensure you remain at the forefront of this powerful tool's capabilities. Dive in, explore, and keep pushing the boundaries of what you can achieve with Excel.

Made in the USA
Las Vegas, NV
07 February 2025

17686711R00070